Junk Drawer

BIOLOGY

50 AWESOME ACTIVITIES | That Don't Cost a Thing

BOBBY MERCER

CHICAGO
REVIEW
PRESS

Published by Chicago Review Press Incorporated
814 North Franklin Street
Chicago, Illinois 60610
ISBN 978-1-64160-289-1

Library of Congress Cataloging-in-Publication Data
Names: Mercer, Bobby, author.
Title: Junk drawer biology : 50 awesome experiments that don't cost a thing
   / Bobby Mercer.
Description: Chicago : Chicago Review Press, 2020. | Audience: Ages 9 to 12
   | Audience: Grades 4-6 | Summary: "Biology is the study of life, and all
   the wonderful, squishy, messy parts that living things are made of. And
   children love messy science, especially hands-on experimentation! Junk
   Drawer Biology will demonstrate that you don't need high-tech equipment
   to make learning fun-just what you can find in your recycling bin and
   around the house. Aspiring doctors can build a model of human lungs with
   balloons and a soda bottle, and a homemade stethoscope with tubing and
   plastic lid. Budding gardeners will germinate beans and explore how
   leaves "breathe" and "sweat." And all ages will enjoy a double helix
   made of candy. Science educator Bobby Mercer provides readers with
   hands-on experiments to explain the building blocks of living matter for
   children of all ages. The projects can be modified to meet the skill
   levels of the children doing them, from elementary school kids to
   teenagers. Though each challenge includes suggested materials and one
   step-by-step, illustrated solution, children are encouraged to think
   further come up with more questions to answer. Educators and parents
   will find this title a handy resource to teach children while having a
   lot of fun"-- Provided by publisher.
Identifiers: LCCN 2020002756 (print) | LCCN 2020002757 (ebook) | ISBN
   9781641602891 (trade paperback) | ISBN 9781641602907 (pdf) | ISBN
   9781641602914 (mobi) | ISBN 9781641602921 (epub)
Subjects: LCSH: Biology--Juvenile literature.
Classification: LCC QH309.2 .M47 2020 (print) | LCC QH309.2 (ebook) | DDC
   570--dc23
LC record available at https://lccn.loc.gov/2020002756
LC ebook record available at https://lccn.loc.gov/2020002757

Cover design: Andrew Brozyna
Interior design: Sadie Teper
Interior photos: Bobby Mercer

Printed in the United States of America
5 4 3 2 1

To Team Science: Jennifer Allsbrook,
Shannon Haynes, and Leslie Rhinehart.

Thanks for inspiring students every day.

Contents

Acknowledgments

Books don't happen without great people helping along the way. Thanks to Kathy Green, the best agent in the business. Thanks to Jerome Pohlen and the gifted people at Chicago Review Press for making this book a reality. Thanks to the wonderful people I work with; their thoughts, ideas, and encouragement mean the world to me. Shannon Haynes, Jennifer Allsbrook, Ethan Abbott, and Leslie Rhinehart have been invaluable shoulders to lean on. To Brandon Schweitzer, Josh Hill, Michelle Bean, and Aaron Greene, thanks for being supportive in all the right ways. As always, thanks to my wonderful better half, Michele, and my two partners in hands-on mayhem, Nicole and Jordan.

Introduction

Biology is the study of life. A living thing is anything that breathes, eats, grows, and dies. Plants, animals, bacteria, fungi, and more meet this criterion. Life is precious, whether it is a simple flower or a beautiful baby.

From the simple to the complex, life is also fun to learn about. Your amazing body is a great place to start. All the parts and pieces of your body are complex. Your body never stops. Your heart, lungs, and brain keep working even when you are asleep.

Plants and animals bring us so much joy. Pets make us smile and laugh. Flowers brighten our lives. Plants and animals (and you) are made up of cells. The cell is an incredible powerhouse that keeps us alive and keeps flowers growing.

The activities in this book make use of things you probably already have around the house. Play with Play-Doh to learn how cells grow and reproduce. Turn a chicken bone into rubber. Dissolve the shell off an egg and make it glow.

So, open your junk drawer and learn some biology.

1

Human Body

The human body is more powerful than any computer. It controls every waking (and sleeping) minute of your life. The bones, blood, muscles, and all the organs in your body keep you running, jumping, and playing.

Have fun, enjoy these activities, and learn more about your incredible body.

Dominant Eye

You know that you are right-handed or left-handed, but do you also know you are right-eyed or left-eyed?

Biology Concept: Eye dominance

From the Junk Drawer:

☐ Sticky note (or any relatively small object you can place on a wall, like a clock)

Step 1: Place the sticky note or other chosen object on a wall. Make a triangle with right and left thumbs and index fingers and hold them out in front of you. With both eyes open, center the sticky note (or object) in the triangle. You should be at least 10 feet away from the sticky note.

Step 2: Close your left eye. If the object is still in the triangle, your right eye is dominant. Now close your right eye. If the object is still in the triangle, your left eye is dominant. Alternate closing each eye and watch the object move in and out of the triangle. Depending on the size of the distant object, it may only move part of the way out of the triangle with the dominant eye closed.

The Science Behind It

Like most people, you know if you are right-handed or left-handed—you have a dominant hand. But you also have a dominant eye. That means the image from that eye plays a greater role in your brain as it creates a complete picture of what you are looking at.

Knowing which eye is dominant is important in sports like baseball and softball. You want to turn your head so that your dominant eye sees more of the ball movement. It is also important in photography with fancy cameras. Since only one eye can look through the viewfinder, you want it to be the dominant eye. Because the image from the dominant eye will remain fairly clear even with different input from your other eye, you can keep both eyes open as you shoot the photographs. This allows you to see things outside the viewfinder, like people walking into the scene, a bird you might want to photograph before it flies away, or a curb you don't want to trip over.

Science for the Ages

This is a great activity for kids of all ages. In a group setting, you could collect data comparing eye dominance and hand dominance. There is a correlation most of the time—right-handed people often have right-eye dominance, and left-handed people are often left-eye dominant. You can also research eye dominance on the internet with permission.

Blind Spot

Try this blind spot activity to learn one benefit of having two eyes.

Biology Concepts: Blind spot and how vision works

From the Junk Drawer:

☐ Index card
☐ Marker
☐ Colored dot sticker (or colored thumbtack)

Step 1: Mark an X and place a colored dot sticker on an index card as shown. You can also use a colored thumbtack. You can simply draw a circle in lieu of a sticker, but the addition of color makes it more obvious.

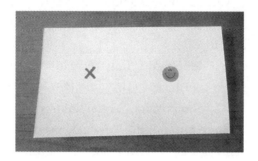

Step 2: Hold the card about 18 inches in front of your face—this is the length of one and a half standard rulers. Cover your left eye with your hand. Look at the X with your right eye. Keep your eye focused on the X the entire time.

Step 3: Slowly move the card toward your face. At one point, the sticker will disappear from your view. Stop the card at this location. Then move it slightly backward or forward, and it will reappear.

Step 4: Rotate the card so that the X and sticker have swapped places and repeat Steps 2 and 3 for the other eye. Cover the right eye and have your left eye focus on the X. The colored sticker will again disappear.

The Science Behind It

When you look at something, your eye lens focuses an image onto the **retina** inside your eye. The rods and cones in your eye's retina act like the electronic device in a camera that captures pictures. Rods and cones detect an image and send electric signals to your brain through the optic nerve. There is a small area with no rods or cones where the optic nerve leaves your retina.

In this Blind Spot activity, the image of the sticker is projected on that spot. Your brain automatically fills in that area with the surrounding picture. You see the white of the index card, but no color. Both of your eyes have a blind spot. With both eyes open, you never have a blind spot because your brain combines the image from each eye, filling in the missing pieces, so you see everything.

Science for the Ages

This is appropriate for all ages. This a fun activity to generate interest in how the eye works.

Hole in Your Hand

Learn one component of how sight works.
Biology Concept: Vision

From the Junk Drawer:

☐ Paper   ☐ Tape

Step 1: Roll a piece of paper into a tube and secure it with a small piece of
tape. The photo shows dark tape, but any tape will do.

Step 2: Hold the tube in front of one eye and look through it. Make sure the
tube is all the way against your face. Keep both eyes open. Now place your
other hand next to the middle of the tube as shown. What do you see?

Step 3 Now switch hands and repeat the activity. Did one eye work better than the other?

The Science Behind It

Your eyes act independent of one another, but your brain puts the images they see together. Your brain makes assumptions about what you see. Normally, both eyes are focusing on the same object and see the same thing. But in this case, one eye sees your hand and the other eye sees a small tunnel. When your brain puts the images together, you appear to have a hole in your hand. Because you have a dominant eye, this effect will appear clearer when looking through the tube with your dominant eye.

Science for the Ages

This is a great introduction to eyesight. It also serves as a great Fun Science Friday activity. Fun Science Friday is a great way for science teachers to add an enjoyable end to the week. In my classroom, almost every Friday, we do a fun hands-on activity. Preschool students will need some help to realize what they are seeing. Elementary age and up are always amazed by this; high school students love it.

Little Baby Carrot Finger

See a floating finger and learn about your eyes.

Biology Concept: **Binocular vision**

From the Junk Drawer:

☐ Two fingers

Step 1: Bend your arms at about a 90-degree angle and put your two index
    fingers together as shown and look at an object on the other side of the
    room, such as a clock or a picture. Raise your arms so that you have to look
    just past your fingers to watch the object. Focus on the distant object and
    not your fingers. What do you see?

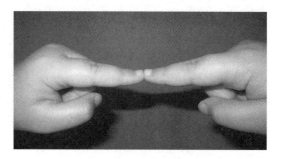

Step 2: Now, continue looking at the distant object but pull your fingers
    slightly part. What do you see now? I call this the Little Baby Carrot
    Finger. Move your fingers back and forth a little as you look at the distant
    object and watch the baby carrot grow and shrink.

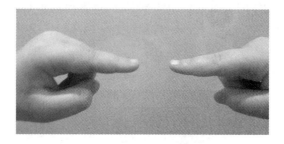

The Science Behind It

This fun optical illusion is caused by binocular rivalry. Normally when we look at something, our eyes angle inward slightly and meet at the surface of the object. How much our eyes angle in gives us depth perception. Depth perception tells our brains how far something is away from us.

In this Little Baby Carrot Finger activity, you are looking beyond the object (the fingers) and looking at a wall. Your brain is now presented with two similar images but doesn't put them together correctly. So, you see the tips of both fingers floating in the air between your other two fingers. The competing images confuse your brain.

Science for the Ages

This a fun activity for all ages. For teachers, it is a gee-whiz activity to grab their attention. It also makes a great filler if you have five minutes left in class.

Upside Down Eyeball

Use a pinhole lens to show how our eyes work.

Biology Concept: Images on your retina

Adult supervision required

From the Junk Drawer:

☐ Small plastic or paper cup
☐ Pushpin
☐ Wax paper (or tissue)

☐ Rubber band (or tape)
☐ Candle or lamp

Step 1: Use a pushpin to create a small hole in the bottom of a paper cup.

Step 2: Wrap a thin piece of wax paper tight around the open end of the cup. A piece of tissue will also work. Secure it in place using a rubber band (or tape).

Step 3: Light a candle with adult permission. You can also use a lamp if you remove the shade. Aim the pinhole at the candle (or light bulb). Look at the waxed paper tissue (or tissue). What do you see? Look at the point of the flame. What do you see?

Step 4 (optional): You can also do this with a window on a sunny day. Turn off all the lights in the room. Aim the pinhole at the window and see what appears on the tissue.

The Science Behind It

Your eye has a lens that allows you to focus on different things. A small pinhole also acts like a lens. As the light passes through this pinhole, the "lens" flips the image over. The image is projected on the tissue paper, but it is upside down. Your eye does the same thing. When you look at a tall tree, the picture on the inside of your eye is upside down. Your brain flips the picture over because your brain knows the sky and the leaves are at the top of the picture. Everything you have ever looked at is upside down on your retina.

The inside of your eye is called the retina and is covered with rods and cones. Rods and cones pick up the light and color of the image that is created on the retina. This information is sent to your brain to process the image. Your brain flips the image over without you having to do anything.

Science for the Ages

This is fun for all ages and will help students understand eyesight. In a classroom, this is a great introduction to the senses. Waxed paper is more durable and easier for little fingers (and big fingers).

Movie Time

Learn how television and movies work.

Biology Concept: Persistence of vision

From the Junk Drawer:

☐ Paper towel tube (or toilet paper
   tube)

☐ Marker

☐ Scissors

☐ Tape

☐ Dark scrap paper

Step 1: Draw a circle onto the scrap paper by tracing around one end of the
   paper towel or toilet paper tube

Step 2: Cut out the circle.

Step 3: Cut the circle in half.

Step 4: Tape one half of the circle over the end of the tube. You will need several pieces of tape to hold it in place.

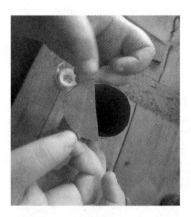

Step 5: Place the other piece over the other side leaving a 2 or 3 mm slit between the two sides. Tape in place.

Step 6: Hold the tube with the open end in front of your eye. Close your other eye and cover it with your hand to block out all external light. Hold the tube still and look at something. You will not be able to see much. Now move your head quickly around the entire room with the tube still held up to your eye You actually can see most of the room even though you only get a small sliver of information at a time.

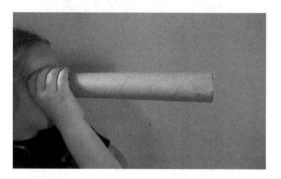

The Science Behind It

Your brain can hold onto an image you see for 1/30 of a second. This image is stored in your brain for that long. If the image is replaced with a similar image, the transition between images is not noticeable. So, when you move your head fast enough, you brain can create an entire picture of the room.

Movies and television take advantage of this persistence of vision. A movie is just a series of still images that quickly replace each other, giving the appearance of motion. For years, the standard refresh rate for television and movies was 24 times per second, and most individual images were shown at least twice during that time. This allowed your brain to "see" seamless motion.

Newer television, movies, and computer monitors refresh at a much faster rate. When you stop a television picture (or movie), you see a single image. The continual replacement of single images looks like motion because of your persistence of vision.

Science for the Ages

This is suitable for all ages.

Blink and You Might Miss It

Explore the blink **reflex** with your friends.

Biology Concept: Blink reflex

From the Junk Drawer:

☐ Recycled paper

☐ Clear window (or any transparent material)

☐ Friend

Step 1: Have a friend stand behind a see-through barrier. A window works well, but a screen door will also work. Clear report covers, transparencies, or the large flat top of a vegetable tray from the produce department are also great choices.

Roll up a ball of recycled paper. Toss the paper at your friend's face. Did your friend blink? Switch places and repeat.

The Science Behind It

The blink reflex is also called the corneal reflex. The **cornea** is the covering of your eyeball. The reflex is designed to protect your eye from being struck. The reflex occurs in about 1/10 of a second.

Your eye also has an optical reflex, which causes you to squint quickly when you are suddenly exposed to a bright light. This reflex is slower. You squint because your pupils are dilated (open), and they need a bit of time to adjust and contract.

All reflexes are involuntary. That means they will happen whether you want them to or not. A common reflex you have probably been tested for is the knee-jerk reflex, called the patellar reflex. This test is usually done by a doctor hitting just below your kneecap with a rubber-tipped hammer. The test is checking how the nerve signals work in your lower spine.

Science for the Ages

This is a great activity to begin a discussion of the nervous system. You can also test a group of people to see if it affects everybody. In a classroom setting, transparencies (or old report covers) are great tools that make it easy to do this activity as a class. The students will enjoy it and stay motivated to listen to the rest of the discussion, and the transparencies can be used year after year.

Shine a Light

Discover why your pupil dilates and also why doctors shine a light in your eye at their office.

Biology Concept: Pupil response to light

From the Junk Drawer:

☐ Magnifying mirror   ☐ Small flashlight

Step 1: This activity works best with a magnifying mirror. Makeup and compact mirrors are slightly curved, which makes the image of your eye much larger. Slowly move the magnifying mirror away from your eye until you see a magnified image of just one of your eyes. What do you see? Pay attention to the pupil, the dark part that is surrounded by the colored part of your eye. Now, find a dark room in your house to do Steps 2 and 3.

Step 2: For this step, use a small flashlight. A keychain flashlight is perfect for this, but any small flashlight will work. It is best if the flashlight is not too bright. (The picture below was taken with a larger flashlight to show the correct position of the light beam.)

Turn on the small flashlight and hold it in the hand not holding the magnifying glass. Place the flashlight next to the mirror. Aim the beam of light by the side of your cheek but not in your eye. Hold it for about 30 seconds, so your pupil will open (dilate).

Step 3: Slowly move the flashlight so it shines in your open eye. This may be a little uncomfortable the first time, but it is not dangerous. What happens to your pupil when you move the beam of light onto it? Now, move it away and watch what happens. Wait 30 seconds between each trial, so your pupil can relax and then open wide. (The second picture below shows the activity being done with a keychain flashlight.)

The Science Behind It

The dark center part of your eye is called the pupil. The pupil allows light to reach the retina (inside lining) of your eye. This pupil can open and close depending on how much light is present.

Your pupil opens and closes to prevent your eyes from being damaged by too much light. It will contract as the light becomes very bright. You may have even seen the pupil contract too much when the light first hit it. It will expand back to what works best for your brain. As you remove the flashlight away, the pupil will open back up to how it was before.

Most pupils contract faster than they expand. You notice this effect when you go outside of your house on a bright summer day. Your pupils almost instantly start to contract and, if it is bright enough, you will actually squint for a few seconds. When you turn the lights off in your room at night, it will appear very dark at first because your pupil opening is very small. But after about 30 seconds, your pupils will have fully opened, and you will see more of the stuff in your room.

Science for the Ages

This activity is fine for all ages if the flashlight is not too strong. In a classroom or partnered homeschool setting, you can skip the mirror. If you have it, a magnifying glass may help the students see the light's effect on the eye better. Pair the students up. Have one person look through the magnifying lens to see his or her partner's giant eye image. Have the first student slowly shine the light in the other student's pupil and watch the result. This is best done in a dark room. Have the students switch places, so both partners can see it.

What Big Ears You Have

Create funnels to hear better.

Biology Concept: Hearing

From the Junk Drawer:

- ☐ Paper plates
- ☐ Heavy scrap paper (like construction paper or a magazine cover)
- ☐ Tape
- ☐ Scissors
- ☐ Radio, television, or friends for a source of sound

Step 1: Cut 1/4 out of a paper plate as shown.

Step 2: Cut a small circle out of the middle of the larger part of the plate you have left. You are creating a pinna, which is the name for the outer part of your ear. Repeat Steps 1 and 2 to create a second pinna. These are going to slide behind your ears, and because the skin there is sensitive, you might want to add tape along the cut edge of the paper plates.

Step 3 Turn toward the source of sound. You could just have a friend continuously talk, or you could play music (or television). First listen to the sound without the plates. Turn your head slowly around to see if the sound level changes. Did the sound get louder or softer?

Now place your hands behind your ears and cup them forward. Again, turn your head and listen to how the sound changes. What happens when you are turned toward a sound? What happens when the sound is behind you?

Step 4: Now place the paper-plate pinnae behind your ears and cup them forward. Turn your head again and listen to how the sound changes. What happens when you are facing the sound? What happens when it is behind you?

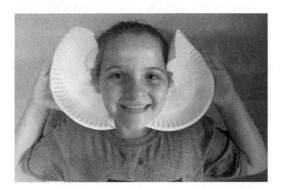

Step 5: Now lay the pinnae back against the side of your ears, like elephant's ears. Turn your head again. Does the sound change this time?

Step 6: You are now going to create an ear trumpet. Take a piece of scrap paper and roll it up into a cone. Cut off the pointy end to make it flat, making sure the end is too large to fit entirely inside your ear canal. Hold that end near your ear and turn your head to the sound. How does the ear trumpet help?

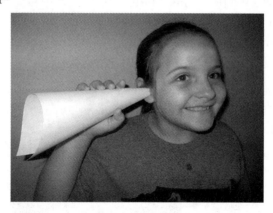

The Science Behind It

The pinnae are the outer parts of your ears. They funnel sounds into your ear canal. The ear canal captures the sounds and funnels them to your eardrum. The eardrum moves with the air pressure difference and helps your brain hear the sound. The pinnae not only funnel the sounds, they also block sounds coming from other directions. The bigger your outer ear is, the better you can hear.

What animal has the biggest ears? Elephants have gigantic ears, but they don't help them hear better. Elephant ears are large to help them keep cool. Blood running through their ears is close to the surface of their skin. The blood is warm but loses heat to the surrounding air. This carries heat away and cools the elephant. They can also flap them like a fan to cool themselves off.

The ear trumpet in the final step was similar to the earliest hearing aids. Thomas Edison used one late in his life. Modern hearing aids use an amplifier to make the sound louder. They sit at the end of your ear canal and amplify sound.

Science for the Ages

This is perfect for all ages if the safety measures are followed.

Inflation to Breathe

Using bottles, straws, and balloons to build a model of lungs.

Biology Concepts: Breathing and how your lungs work

Adult supervision required

From the Junk Drawer:

☐ Plastic drink bottle
☐ Flexible straw
☐ Tape
☐ Scissors
☐ Hot glue gun
☐ Marker
☐ Three balloons

Step 1: Mark about 2/3 of the way down a plastic drink bottle as shown. Thicker bottles work better, so avoid very thin plastic water bottles. Ask an adult to use a sharp knife to cut a small slit in the bottle along the marked line.

Step 2: Slide the point of a pair of scissors into the slit and cut around the bottle.

Step 3: With adult help, use the point of the scissors to start creating a hole in the bottle cap. Spinning the cap will make it easier to dig the hole. The straw needs to fit tightly through the hole, so test it several times as you widen the hole until it is a tight fit.

Step 4: Extend the flexible part of the straw and slightly bend it. Use the scissors to cut a small slot in the flexible part. Next, cut about two inches off the longer straight part of the straw.

Step 5: Cut at an angle on the two-inch piece as shown. Insert the angled end of the small two-inch piece into the slot in the flexible part of the straw. You want it to be a tight fit. Trim the opening if needed.

Step 6: With adult help, use a hot glue gun to seal the point where the straws come together. The easiest way is to seal one side and then flip it over to seal the other. Trim the branching ends of the "Y" to make the straw parts an equal length. Leave the single end of the Y longer than the two branches.

Step 7: Cut the neck off two balloons.

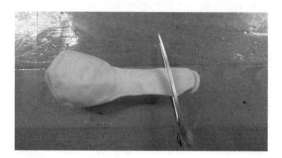

Step 8: Slide one balloon over one branch of the Y. Use tape to seal the balloon to the straw. Attach the other balloon to the other branch of the straw in the same way.

Step 9: Put the cap on the bottle and tighten it. Slide the single, longer end of the Y through the hole in the bottle cap. The two branches of the Y and the balloons should be on the bottom side of the cap, inside the plastic bottle. Use the hot glue gun to seal around the opening on the top of the bottle cap. You can trim the top of the Y to just above the cap.

Step 10: Make a cut across the middle of another balloon.

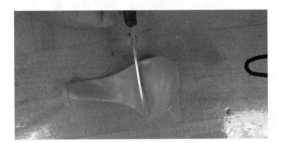

Step 11: Stretch the balloon opening over the bottom of your bottle, then tape around the edge of the balloon to hold it in place. Your finished lung set should look like the picture below.

Step 12: Pull on the bottom of the balloon to use your lung model. See how the "lungs" inflate as you pull down on the balloon stretched over the bottom of the bottle and deflate as you let the balloon fall back to its original position. How much the lungs inflate depends on how airtight your seals are, but you should see some movement.

The Science Behind It

You have created a small model of your respiratory system. Your lungs are represented by the two balloons inside the bottle. The upper part of the Y represents the trachea. The trachea is connected to your nose and mouth. You get air in and out of your body by using your trachea. The bottom balloon represents your diaphragm. As your diaphragm contracts, it "pulls down" (like the balloon in Step 12) and makes your chest cavity larger. This causes air to be pulled into your lungs, making your lungs expand. As the diaphragm relaxes, air will rush out of your lungs and cause them to deflate. Inside your lungs, oxygen (from outside air) is transferred into your bloodstream, which keeps your **cells** alive. The lungs, trachea, and diaphragm are part of your respiratory system.

Some animals only have a single lung and breathe using their cheeks instead of their diaphragm.

Science for the Ages

This activity is appropriate for elementary students and up. Special care needs to be taken with the hot glue gun and the initial slit in the bottle.

Pump Up the Volume

Build a miniature heart valve model and pump fake blood.

Biology Concepts: Heart pumping and heart valves

From the Junk Drawer:

- ☐ Balloon
- ☐ Scissors
- ☐ Empty plastic jar
- ☐ Water
- ☐ Toothpick
- ☐ 2 flexible straws
- ☐ Tape
- ☐ Pan to catch water

Step 1: Cut off the neck of a balloon near the fat part, as shown.

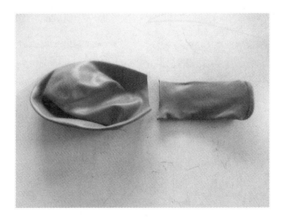

Step 2: Fill an empty plastic jar about 2/3 full of water. The water will be your fake blood. Stretch the fat part of the balloon over the top of an empty plastic jar. Pull the balloon tight, but a few wrinkles are OK. Use a toothpick to poke two tiny holes in the balloon about one inch apart. Slide a straw through each hole. It helps to twist the straw as you are pushing it through.

Step 3: Bend the flexible part of each straw so that their upper sections point slightly downward.

Step 4: Slide the neck of the balloon over one of the straws. Leave at least one inch of the neck beyond the end of the straw. Use tape to seal one end of the neck to the straw. The neck of the balloon will represent a heart valve.

Step 5: Bend the straw with the balloon down and bend the other up. Place the entire heart apparatus in a baking or casserole pan to catch the blood.

Step 6: With two fingers, push down on the balloon stretched over the top of the jar. What happens? Repeat several more times.

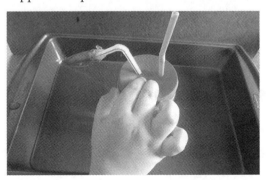

The Science Behind It

Your heart pumps blood all the time. Your heart pumps about 1,500 gallons every day. Your heart contracts and sends blood to your body or to other parts of your heart. When you press on the balloon, you're imitating what your heart muscle does when it contracts. It pumps blood through the valve. The loose neck of the balloon will allow the blood to flow one way but will close to prevent blood from going back to where it just left. Another way to think of a heart valve is a trash can with a flap lid. You can put the trash in, and then the flap closes.

Your heart has four valves and four chambers. The four valves operate in pairs and create the *lubb-dupp* sound of your heartbeat. The *lubb* sound is created by the tricuspid and mitral valves closing. These are the smaller valves that control blood flow between the top and bottom chambers of your heart. The louder *dupp* sound is created by the larger aortic and pulmonary valves. These valves control blood flow to your body and to your lungs. These valves open and close every time your heart beats. Doctors can even put artificial valves if your heart valves start to go bad.

A common defect is a heart murmur. A heart murmur is when the valve doesn't completely close. A small amount of blood will keep moving between the *lubb-dupp* sounds. This can be heard by a trained listener with a stethoscope. It is one of the reasons that doctors listen to your heartbeat every time you go to see them.

Science for the Ages

This works for all ages. You can also pump the heart faster to show what happens when you are exercising and need to move blood faster.

The Hardest Working Muscle

Learn about your heart, an amazing muscle.

Biology Concept: The heart as a muscle

From the Junk Drawer:

☐ Old tennis ball   ☐ Red marker (optional)

☐ Stopwatch (or cell phone)

Step 1: For a fun option, draw a red heart on your tennis ball with a permanent marker. Dry erase markers will be permanent on the tennis ball.

Step 2: Your heart is a muscle, and when it contracts, blood is sent to all parts of your body. It takes about the same amount of force for the heart to contract as it does for a human hand to squeeze an old tennis ball. New tennis balls are harder to squeeze—you could still use them, but you may need two hands. You may need to use both hands on an old tennis ball, too, but that is OK. Place the tennis ball in your hand (or both hands) and start the stopwatch.

Step 3: Squeeze the tennis ball to simulate your heart beating. See how many times you can squeeze it in 60 seconds. Are you tired?

The Science Behind It

At the center of the cardiovascular system is the heart. It is the hardest working and most important muscle in your body. It beats continuously, every day, whether you are awake or asleep. It is a muscle that acts as a pump to move blood through your body. When you exercise, it beats faster. It is very important that you strengthen this muscle by getting exercise. Take care of your heart, and it will take care of you. Get exercise and eat right, and you will lead a long and healthy life.

A heart attack is when blood flow to the outside of the heart muscle stops. This results in part of the muscle dying. It is often just a small part, and with medical help, the heart attack is not fatal. In medical television shows, you often see the doctors and nurses shock a heart with a defibrillator machine. The two paddles are placed on the side and top of the chest. The machine shocks the heart, causing the muscle to contract. The hope is that the heart will then start beating on its own.

A pacemaker is a portable device implanted in the chest that keeps the heart beating as it should.

Science for the Ages

This activity is perfect for all ages. In a classroom setting, you might be able to ask a tennis coach to donate old tennis balls. They will work for this activity even if they have not been in use for a long time. This could also be a great activity to send home with the students. The red heart on the ball is sure to draw a question from a friend or a parent. Then the students can explain what they have learned.

Hardworking Heart

See how hard your heart works every day.

Biology Concept: Cardiovascular system

From the Junk Drawer:

☐ Measuring cup   ☐ Scissors

☐ Water   ☐ 2 buckets

☐ Small paper or plastic cup   ☐ Stopwatch, clock, or cell phone

☐ Marker   ☐ Friend (optional)

Step 1: Your heart pumps about 2 ounces (60 ml) of blood every time it contracts. That number will go up to about 3 ounces (90 ml) as you become a teenager and adult.

Fill up a measuring cup with 2 ounces (1/4 of a cup) of water. Pour the 2 ounces into a small paper cup. A small plastic cup will also work, but a paper cup is easier to cut.

Step 2: Use a marker to mark the water level on the cup.

Step 3: Pour the water out and use scissors to cut the cup at the mark.

Step 4: For easy cleanup, the rest of this activity is usually done outside. Fill one of the buckets with water. Place the cup that you have just cut in that bucket. This could also be done inside using a sink. A double kitchen sink is a great option, if you can plug both sink drains.

Set a stopwatch where it can be seen (or have a friend time you). Almost all cell phones have a stopwatch feature, but you could use a normal clock with a second hand. Keep the cell phone (or clock) away from the water, perhaps on a table while the bucket is on the ground.

Step 5: Start the stopwatch and start scooping (about one scoop per second) water from the full bucket to the empty bucket. Keep going for 60 seconds at a steady pace. Stop after 60 seconds.

Step 6: Check at the amount of water in the once empty bucket. That is how much blood your heart pumped in a minute (60 seconds). Your heart is doing that (and more) every minute you have been alive. Now try it again but go faster. This is what happens when you exercise.

The Science Behind It

The cardiovascular system, also called the circulatory system, is an organ system that delivers blood to all parts of your body. The center of the system is the heart. It is a pump that moves blood to all your organs and tissues. This is a sealed system, so the same blood keeps getting used repeatedly. The blood carries oxygen, nutrients, and hormones to all parts of your body. After the blood gives up all its goodies to the cells, it returns to the heart (and lungs) to start the trip again.

Science for the Ages

This is a great introduction to the heart and the cardiovascular system. It is also a fun way to get outside and learn at the same time. For a classroom, you could use several large buckets. Do the activity outside and just have the students dump water on the ground. The teacher could be the timer for the entire class. It is also a great activity for "water day", since it combines water fun and learning. Many preschools and elementary schools have a water day before school gets out for the summer. Various water-themed activities help make learning fun.

Rubber Bones

Use vinegar and a chicken leg to create a rubber bone and learn what makes healthy bones strong.

Biology Concept: Strong bones

From the Junk Drawer:

☐ Chicken bone   ☐ Glass cup

☐ Small bowl   ☐ Vinegar

Step 1: The next time you eat chicken, keep a leg or thigh bone. Run it under water and clean off as much chicken junk as possible—all you want is the bone. Let the clean bone dry for a few days in a bowl in the refrigerator. Then pull the bone out and try to bend it. Your goal is not to break the bone but to see how strong it is.

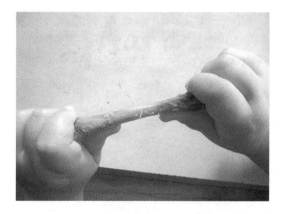

Step 2: Put the bone in a glass cup and fill the cup with vinegar. Make sure the entire bone is covered. Put the glass in a suitable location out of direct sunlight, perhaps a storage room to avoid a heavy vinegar smell in the house. Check the bone once a day for a week. You are looking to see how much you can bend the bone. You can speed up the process if you change the vinegar every day, but it is not required.

Step 3: It usually takes three to five days to get a completely rubber bone, so keep checking. After five days, you can dry the bone and play with it. Show it off to your friends.

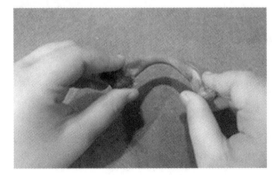

The Science Behind It

The strength of bones comes from calcium. But bones also contain collagen, which is a fibrous protein that gives the bones strength and flexibility. If bones were made only of calcium, they would be brittle and break easily. The collagen gives a framework to the calcium.

The acetic acid in vinegar dissolves the calcium and leaves the chicken bone with only collagen. Soda also contains acid and would do the same thing to a chicken bone, but it would take a few more days. Your teeth are almost entirely made of calcium, so drinking a lot of soda could dissolve that calcium and rot your teeth.

Science for the Ages

This is fun and appropriate for all ages. Some people are bothered by the vinegar smell, so a well-ventilated area is a good idea. You could try several different acids and see which is fastest. Different sodas, tea, and lemonade could all be compared.

Flexible Spine

Use a straw and a pipe cleaner to build your own backbone.

Biology Concepts: Spine, vertebrae, and spinal cord

From the Junk Drawer:

☐ Pipe cleaner
☐ Nonflexible straw
☐ Scissors

Step 1: Slide a pipe cleaner through a straw. Hold the two ends of the pipe cleaner and try to bend it. Don't kink the straw. (You would not want a kink in your spine!) Feel how difficult it is to bend it in the long piece of straw.

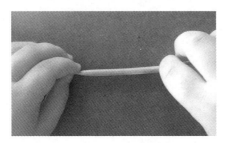

Step 2: Now pull the pipe cleaner out. Use scissors to cut the straw into smaller pieces (about 1/2 inch long).

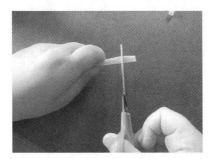

Step 3: Slide the small pieces back over the pipe cleaner. Hold the ends or bend them, so the pieces don't slide off. Now try to bend the pipe cleaner. It is much easier now. The pipe cleaner represents your spinal cord. The small pieces of straw are just like your vertebrae, forming a flexible spine.

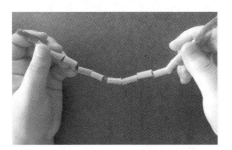

The Science Behind It

You have just built a simple model of your spine, commonly called the backbone. The backbone is actually composed of 33 different bones, but some are fused together. The individual vertebrae are similar to your straw pieces. They protect the spinal cord from damage. The spinal cord is the main way that nerve impulses get to your brain. Individual nerves come out in all directions between each vertebra (or fused sets of vertebrae).

The top seven vertebrae connect the base of your skull to the top of your shoulders. These are called the cervical vertebrae. For doctors, they are numbered C1 at the top to C7 at the bottom of your neck. The next 12 are called the thoracic vertebrae and are located behind your rib cage. They are connected to your ribs. T1 is at the top back of your ribcage and T12 is at the bottom. The next five are called your lumbar vertebrae and are numbered L1 through L5. These are the vertebrae in your lower back. The sacrum is next, and it is actually composed of five vertebrae that are fused together to act as a single bone. At the bottom is the coccyx, which is made up of three fused vertebrae. This is commonly called the tailbone.

Science for the Ages

This is a great introduction for all ages to the spinal cord and vertebrae. Older students could count and label the individual vertebrae to help learn the numbering system.

Rubber Muscles

Build a human arm model with rubber bands to show how muscles work.

Biology Concepts: Muscles and the bones in your arm.

From the Junk Drawer:

☐ Thin cardboard (like a cereal box) ☐ Glue

☐ Pen or marker ☐ Brads (also called paper fasteners)

☐ Scissors ☐ 2 rubber bands

☐ Hole punch ☐ Paper clips

☐ Craft sticks

Step 1: Cut three 3/4-inch by 5-inch strips of thin cardboard. On two of the strips, mark three dots equally spaced near one end as shown. On the third, at each end, make a mark about a 1/2 inch from each end.

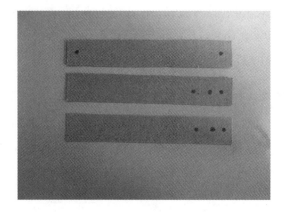

Step 2: Stack the two three-dot strips together. Use several paper clips to hold them together. Punch out all three dots in both strips. These two strips will represent the two bones of your lower arm, called the radius and ulna. Also, punch out the marks on each end of the third strip.

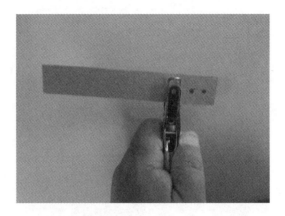

Step 3: Glue a craft stick between the holes on the single leftover strip. White glue or hot glue works fine, but white glue will take longer to dry—about two hours. If the craft stick is too long, you can usually cut it with kitchen shears (and an adult's help).

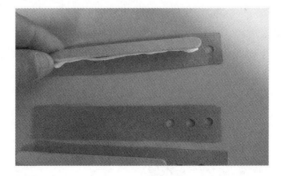

Step 4: Now glue the other craft stick between the two lower arm bones, as shown. Make sure the stick does not cover any of the three holes. It is OK if the craft stick extends past the other end of the cardboard strip. Glue one side down and then flip the other arm bone on top of it.

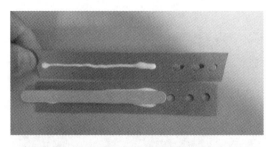

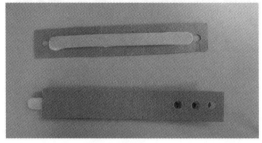

Step 5: Sandwich the upper arm bone between the two lower arm bones. Use a brad (or paper clip) in the middle hole of the three to join the three bones together. Bend the back ends of the brad twice to make them smaller. The lower arm bones should move freely around the brad. The brad represents your elbow.

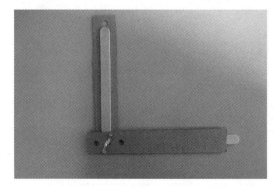

Step 6: Put brads in the remaining three holes. Leave these slightly loose, since you will be tucking rubber bands behind them. Bend the backs of the brads twice to make them smaller.

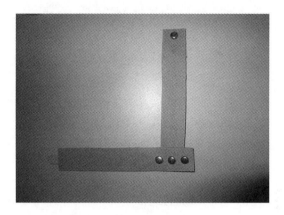

Step 7: Loop a rubber band over the top brad. Place the other end over the brad behind the elbow. This rubber band represents the triceps muscle, which is on the back of your arm. With only a single rubber band on, the arm will bend slightly, rather than staying in place. That is OK.

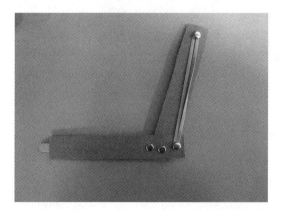

Step 8: Repeat with another rubber band over the top brad and the brad in front of the elbow. This represents the biceps.

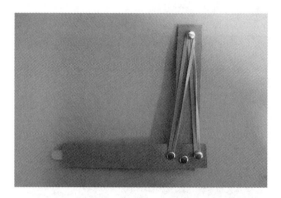

Step 9: When the biceps contracts, the lower arm will curl up toward the upper bone. You can do this by pulling on the biceps rubber band. The triceps rubber band will be relaxed during this curl.

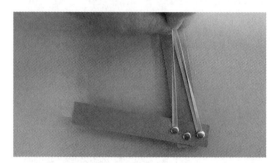

Step 10: Now pull on the triceps rubber band to make it contract. The biceps rubber band will be relaxed. The lower arm will now extend away from the upper arm bone. This is how your biceps and triceps move your arm.

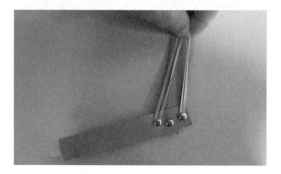

Step 11: Label the three bones to help you remember them. You don't have a thumb on your model, but on your actual arm, the radius is the lower arm bone on the thumb side of your arm. For this craft, you can choose either side to be the radius. Label this bone. Flip the arm over and label the other lower arm bone as the ulna. The upper arm should then be labeled the humerus.

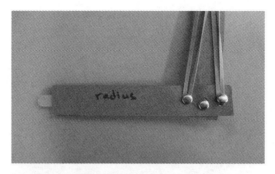

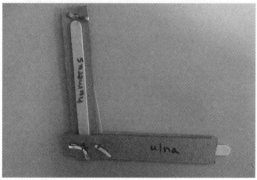

The Science Behind It

The biceps and triceps of your arm are called an antagonistic pair of muscles. When your biceps contracts, it is called an agonistic muscle. It is the muscle that is doing the work. The triceps becomes an antagonist muscle and relaxes. When the triceps contracts to extend your arm, the roles reverse. The triceps is the agonist (doing the work), and the biceps becomes the antagonist (relaxing muscle).

Another example of an antagonistic muscle pair in your body is your hamstrings and quadriceps. The quadriceps (on the fronts of your legs) are used to extend your leg. The hamstrings (on the backs of your legs) are used to curl your legs up toward your butt.

Science for the Ages

This activity is appropriate for all ages. It can be done with tongue depressors, but you will need an adult to drill the holes. If done with tongue depressors, it could be taken apart and reused in future years. But since the materials are cheap, it is also a wonderful project to send home with children.

That Tastes Great

Taste without smelling or seeing.

Biology Concepts: Olfactory organ and taste buds

From the Junk Drawer:

☐ Bag of jelly beans   ☐ Pencil

☐ 3 plastic bags   ☐ Blindfold (optional)

☐ Sticky notes

Note: This activity was designed so it could be done alone, but working with a partner (or two) might make it more fun.

Step 1: Take a bag of jelly beans and separate the flavor colors into different piles, each pile a different flavor. Select three colors and put the others back in the bag. Put four or five of each color in separate plastic bags and seal each bag but leave out two or three of each flavor. (You might want to write the flavors down on a sticky note for each bag.)

Step 2: Scramble the loose jelly beans into a single pile. Place the bags and the pile where you can easily find them with your eyes closed.

Step 3: Hold your nose closed very tightly. Close your eyes tight. Reach into the pile and pull out a single jelly bean. No peeking allowed! While keeping your nose and eyes closed, bite it in half and chew the jelly bean. What flavor do you think it is? Open your eyes and look at the half you are still holding. Did you guess correctly? If you are doing it with a partner (or two), you could use a blindfold. Repeat several more times with your eyes and nose closed. Did you get the flavors right each time?

Step 4: With your eyes closed, scramble the plastic bags up. Now lift a bag to your nose while keeping your eyes closed. Open the bag and take a deep smell. What flavor do you think it is? Open your eyes and check. Were you correct? If working with partners, a partner could lift the bag to your nose and write down your guess. Repeat several more times.

The Science Behind It

The taste buds in your mouth allow you to make sense of different tastes, like sweet, salty, bitter, etc. But the olfactory cells in your nose detect smells, and this helps you taste food. All the jelly beans are sweet, but the smell (and color) give you the actual flavor. That is part of the reason why, when your nose is plugged, food doesn't taste as appealing—or as disgusting. This is why my daughter plugs her nose when we make her try a new food, if she thinks it will be nasty.

Science for the Ages

This is a fun activity for all ages. For a healthier alternative, you can use apples and potatoes. If you cut the skin off and make the pieces the same shape, it is very hard to distinguish between the two. In a classroom setting, you can keep all the pieces at the front desk and call up students one at a time. Have them guess while other students write their answers down on the board.

Thumbs Up

Examine your own thumbprint and compare it to others' thumbprints.

Biology Concept: The uniqueness of your thumbprint

From the Junk Drawer:

☐ Pencil   ☐ Smartphone
☐ White paper   ☐ Friend (optional)
☐ Clear tape

Step 1: Hold a pencil to the white paper and angle it so that the side of the
graphite at the end of the pencil is resting on the paper. Move the pencil
back and forth to rub graphite onto the paper in the shape of a rectangle.
Make sure the area is larger than your thumb.

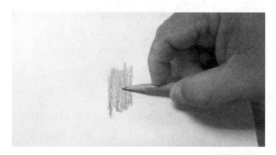

Step 2: Press your thumb down on the graphite smudge. Some of the
graphite will be picked up by your thumbprint.

Step 3: Getting a good thumbprint takes practice, so you might need to do it a few times to get a good one. You can also do another finger if you prefer. Take a four-inch-long piece of clear tape. Lightly wrap it down your thumb with your other hand. This will put your thumbprint on the tape, and the graphite makes it easier to see. Having a friend's help might make this easier, but you can do it by yourself. You can hold one end of the tape up to a light and see if you got a good thumbprint. It may take a few tries to get a good one.

Step 4: Lightly place the tape on a white piece of paper. Be careful: pressing on the center of the tape may destroy the thumbprint. You can press the ends down that were not in contact with your thumb. Examine the prints with a smartphone camera. You can zoom in and take a picture. You can also use the Smartphone Microscope from this book (page 187).

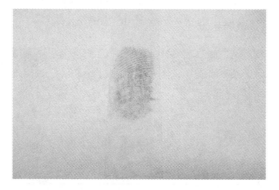

The Science Behind It

Fingerprints are the impressions left by the ridges on your finger. They are unique to every person. They are a series of arches, loops, and whirls created by the friction ridges on your fingers. They are very difficult to alter, and you have the same ones for your entire life. They are one of the primary tools that the police use to identify criminals. You may need to be fingerprinted for a job in your future. Of course, some smartphones already use a thumbprint scanner on your phone. The scanner identifies you by your fingerprint to unlock your phone.

Now police departments and businesses usually use a scanner to get your fingerprints. They used to use ink pads, which was very messy. Your teachers were all probably fingerprinted when they got their first teacher job.

Science for the Ages

This is safe for all ages and easier to clean up than ink. It will take some practice to get a good fingerprint, but little ones can do it.

Cool Me Off

Learn about the purpose of sweat.

Biology Concepts: **Perspiration** and evaporative cooling

From the Junk Drawer:

☐ Water
☐ Your hand

Step 1: Dip one finger into water. Rub that finger on the back of your other hand to get it wet. What does the back of your hand feel like? Does it feel colder than it did before you put the water on it?

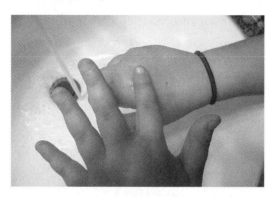

Step 2: Now blow across the wet area on the back of your hand. Does it feel colder than it did in Step 1?

The Science Behind It

Perspiration is a fancy word for sweat. Your body sweats anytime your core temperature starts to go above normal (98.6° F). The hypothalamus in your brain acts like the thermostat in your house. When you get too hot, it activates your **sweat glands** to cool you off.

Sweating cools you off in two ways. First, the sweat on your skin is at a lower temperature and pulls heat out of your body. Second, as sweat evaporates (turning from a liquid to a gas), it carries some of the heat away in its gaseous form.

You have two types of sweat glands in your body: eccrine and apocrine. Eccrine glands are all over your body but are most abundant on your forehead, palms, and soles of your feet. Eccrine glands create clear sweat that has almost no smell. Apocrine glands, on the other hand, are most commonly found where you have hair follicles. Sweat from these glands combine with bacteria already on your skin to produce body odor. Interestingly, the only places that you have no sweat glands are your lips and your ear canals.

Sweat also removes salts from your body. These salts are electrolytes and must eventually be replaced. Electrolytes are in many popular sports drinks. You get enough natural electrolytes most of the time. You only need sports drinks when you are doing very intense exercise.

Science for the Ages

This activity is great for all ages. This activity can be repeated using rubbing alcohol. The rubbing alcohol evaporates faster, so you cool off even faster.

$$P^2 + 2Pq + q^2 = 1$$

$$6CO_2 + 6H_2O \rightarrow C_6H_{12}O_6 + 6O_2$$

$$P + q = 1$$

$$2H_2O \rightarrow 4H^+ + O_2$$

2

Plants and Animals

Biology is not just the study of your body; it is the study of all life. The diverse assortment of plants and animals around us is amazing. Organisms from the smallest bacteria to the largest animal, the blue whale, are living, breathing, and creating a wonderful variety of living things on our planet. These activities will help you dive into the world of plants and animals.

Bird Beaks

Model different bird beaks using household items and practice eating like a bird.

Biology Concepts: Bird beaks and animal adaptation

From the Junk Drawer:

☐ Marshmallows
☐ Paper clips
☐ Rubber bands
☐ Cup
☐ Small scissors

☐ Tweezers
☐ Spoon
☐ Water
☐ Drinking straw

Step 1: Put marshmallows, paper clips, and rubber bands on a table—this is your "food." Hold your "stomach" (the cup) in your off hand.

Now, pick up the small scissors in your other hand—they will be your "beak." For 30 seconds, using only the scissors, try to gather as much food as possible, moving it from the table to the stomach. Don't use your other hand except to hold the stomach—remember, birds don't have hands. What food was the easiest to get with the scissors? Did the scissors cut any of the types of food open?

Step 2: Empty the stomach back onto the table. Now hold the tweezers, your new beak, in your dominant hand, and the stomach (cup) in the other. Pick up as much as you can in 30 seconds. What food is easiest to pick up with the tweezers? Could you pick up two types of things simultaneously with the tweezers?

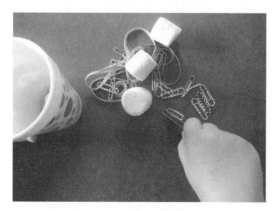

Step 3: Empty your stomach back onto the table. Now use the spoon as your beak. Pick up as much as you can in 30 seconds and place it in the stomach. What food is the easiest to pick up with the spoon? Could the spoon pick up more than one kind of food easier than the scissors or tweezers?

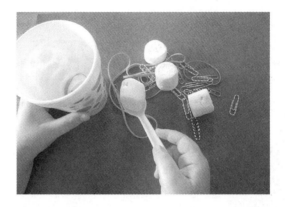

Step 4: Empty your stomach back onto the table. Rinse out the cup or use a new one for the last step. Put some water in it. Now, you are going to use a straw for a beak and the cup will the source of the food. Put the straw in your mouth and try to get some food (water) into your mouth. Do you know of any birds that drink all of their food?

The Science Behind It

Different kinds of birds have different beaks, depending on what type of food they eat. This is an example of adaptation. The birds' beaks have adapted over time to help them survive in their environment. For example, hummingbirds have developed long, thin beaks with a hole in the center like a straw. This straw allows them to drink nectar from a flower (or a hummingbird feeder). Seedeaters (like finches and sparrows) have developed short, hard beaks to break open seeds. Raptors (like hawks and eagles) have developed a hooked end on their beaks to rip open flesh and make bite-sized pieces. Woodpeckers developed a very hard beak to break through the outer bark and wood of a tree to get the insects inside. Pelicans have a large, open bottom to their beaks, almost like a net, that can scoop up fish. Ducks have a similar style of beaks, but they will eat almost anything. They can scoop up fish and fish eggs, but also insects and plants.

The scissors in this activity represented two different types of beaks. If you used them to stab the marshmallows, you mimicked birds that feed on fish, like kingfishers and herons. The scissors could have also helped tear open a marshmallow, just like the beak of an eagle or a hawk would tear open its prey, like mice. The tweezers represented a beak that can pick up seeds to eat, like the beak of a cardinal. The tweezers also represented the beaks of birds that eat worms and insects, like robins and bluebirds, though robins eat almost anything. The spoon could scoop up almost all of the food items, so it resembled the beak of a bird that eats everything, like a duck.

A cool fact about bird beaks is that almost all birds are born with an egg tooth. The egg tooth is a small, tooth-like structure on the top of the upper part of a hatchling's beak. It is used to break the egg open as the bird hatches. The egg tooth generally falls off in a few days, or in some cases, is reabsorbed into the beak.

Also interesting, both parts of the "jaw" in a bird's beak can move, bottom and top. Humans can move only their bottom jaw. The top moves only when the entire skull moves.

Science for the Ages

This is a great introduction to birds and adaptation. For older students, this could be an inquiry-based activity; show the different types of bird beaks and have the students guess what purpose they serve.

Recycled Insect Model

Make an insect from recycled materials.

Biology Concepts: Insect anatomy

From the Junk Drawer:

☐ Empty, rinsed plastic yogurt bottle (or any type of plastic bottle)
☐ Scrap paper

☐ Markers
☐ Scissors
☐ Tape (or glue)

Step 1: Any clean plastic bottle will work for this activity, but the insect shown here was created with a small recycled yogurt bottle. Trace around the mouth of the yogurt bottle on scrap paper. Use a marker to draw eyes and a mouth on the circle and then cut the circle out.

Step 2: Use a long piece of tape to tape over the face to secure it to the top of the bottle. If your bottle has a blank lid, you could just draw a face on the lid. This is the head of your insect.

Step 3: Cut two thin strips of scrap paper. Fold the paper accordion style with two or three folds. These will be your insect's antennae. Tape these to the head of your insect.

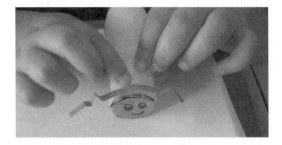

Step 4: Cut three longer strips of paper for the legs. Lay a piece of clear tape on your workspace with the sticky side facing up. Place the legs on the tape as shown.

Step 5: Turn the insect model over. Pick up the ends of tape and attach the legs to the underside of the insect's middle. This middle section is called the thorax.

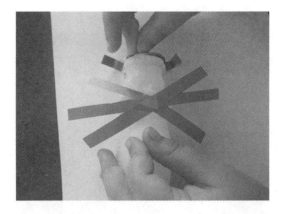

Step 6: You might want to fold the end of each leg. Insects have legs that act much like ours and bend at certain points.

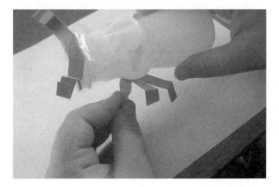

Step 7: Cut two wings out of scrap paper. An easy way to create wigs is to draw a long, skinny heart, then cut the point off the heart. Perhaps use an old magazine or something colorful for the wings. Attach them to the top of the thorax.

Step 8: Now, look at the cute little bug you just made.

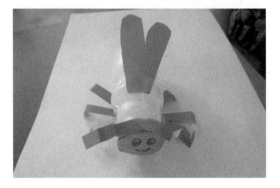

Step 9: To learn more about insects, set your model on a blank piece of paper. Insects have three segments: the head, the thoracic region, and the abdomen. Draw lines between the segments to help you learn the difference.

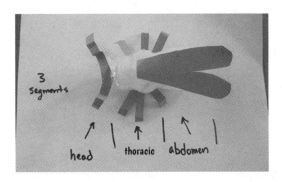

Step 10: Turn the paper over and label the major parts of your insect. This insect has two antennae, six legs, and two wings.

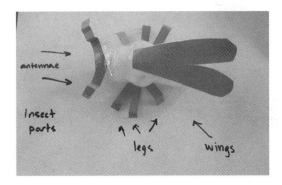

Step 11: Here is another recycled insect created by a nine-year-old. It was made from a thin-walled water bottle that was twisted to separate the thorax from the abdomen.

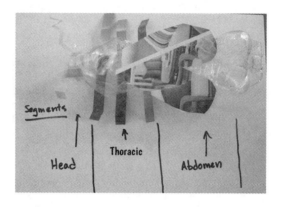

Step 12: This insect also has two antennae, six legs, and two wings, all cut from an old magazine.

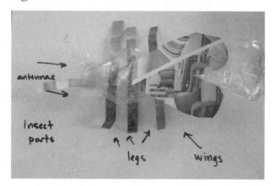

The Science Behind It

Insects are a type of animal. Insects are in the class called Hexapoda—*hex* meaning "six" and *poda* meaning "feet" or "legs," so insects have six legs. All insects also have two antennae, although some are hardly noticeable. Most insects use their antennae to smell. Some insects have wings, but not all. Ants usually do not have wings. A few insects have a stinger, which is located at the back of the abdomen.

The three segments of an insect's body are the head, thorax, and abdomen. The head contains the mouth, eyes, and two antennae. The thorax is the middle section. The legs and wings are connected to the thorax. The abdomen brings up the rear and contains digestive and reproductive organs.

Science for the Ages

This is a great low-cost way to model insects. It also lets little ones be creative. It helps them understand and remember the six legs and three body parts of all the creepy-crawlies that bug them.

Tasty Insect Models

Build a tasty insect from marshmallows.

Biology Concepts: Insect anatomy

From the Junk Drawer:

☐ Marshmallows   ☐ Various candies

☐ Paper   ☐ Pretzels

☐ Toothpicks   ☐ Pen or marker

Step 1: Line up three marshmallows on a piece of clean paper and connect them with toothpicks. These represent the three body segments of all insects: the head, thorax, and abdomen.

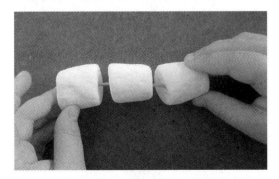

Step 2: The middle section of the insect is called the thorax. This section contains the heart and lungs of the insect. Legs are also attached to this section.

Insects have six legs. Use six pretzels, toothpicks, or pieces of licorice rope to represent the legs.

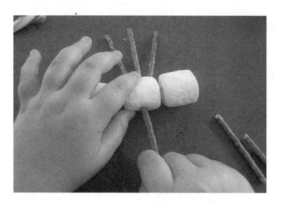

Step 3: The head contains the eyes and antennae. Pick two small candies as eyes. You can use a toothpick to create a hole to keep the candies in place.

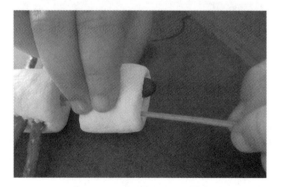

Step 4: Push candy eyes into the holes you created. You could add antennae if you want, using small pieces of licorice rope candy. A toothpick broken in half also makes great antennae.

Step 5: The thorax is where the wings are attached, if the insect has them. Not all insects have wings. Two wrapped lollipops make great wings. Just push them into the middle marshmallow. Sticks of chewing gum or a piece of a fruit roll-up would also make good wings.

Step 6: Admire your scary (and tasty) insect.

Step 7: Place your tasty insect on a piece of paper and label all the parts. And finally—this may be the best part—act like a predator and eat the insect, but remove the toothpicks first.

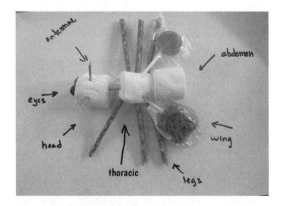

The Science Behind It

Insects make up one of the largest parts of the animal kingdom, from moths and butterflies to ants. All insects have three body parts: the head, thorax, and abdomen. The three body parts are not always the same size, like in this tasty insect project.

Insects also have antennae to inspect the world around them. Most antennae are used to smell, but some insects also use them to help attract a mate. Monarch butterflies even use their antennae to help them migrate.

Having six legs is the telltale sign of an insect. Wings are found on some insects, but not all. Moths and butterflies have them, but most ants do not.

Insects are related to crustaceans, like lobsters and crabs.

Science for the Ages

This activity is appropriate for all ages. You might want to get permission before raiding the candy jar.

The Itsy-Bitsy Tasty Spider

Build a healthy spider and compare it to an insect.

Biology Concepts: Anatomy of a spider and the differences between insects and arachnids

From the Junk Drawer:

☐ Round cheese piece
☐ Toothpicks
☐ Grapes
☐ Pretzels
☐ Paper
☐ Pen or marker

Step 1: Break a toothpick in half. Unwrap a round cheese piece and push the toothpick into one end. You are going to slide a grape onto the toothpick.

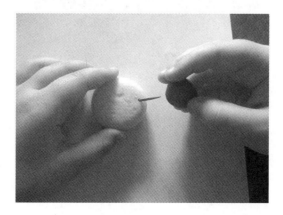

Step 2: Slide the grape all the way down onto the extended toothpick.

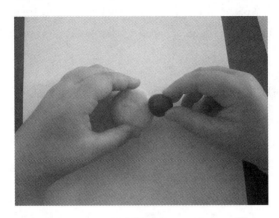

Step 3: The legs can be attached in two ways. The easiest way is to simply slide the pretzels under the cheese. Put four on each side for a total of eight legs. You can also push the pretzels into the cheese, but the cheese will probably break.

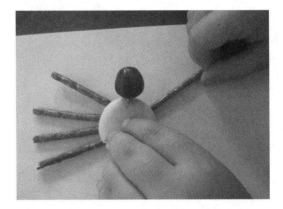

Step 4: Now label the parts to show what you know. The cheese is the body. The grape is the head, and the pretzels are the legs. When you are finished, you get to be a spider predator and devour the spider, but remove the toothpicks first.

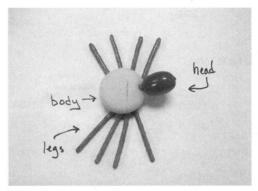

The Science Behind It

Insects and spiders are actually types of animals. They all have segmented bodies and legs with joints, but they also have some differences. Spiders, ticks, and scorpions are called arachnids and have two body segments and eight legs. Insects have three body segments and six legs. Some insects have wings, but no spiders do. Interestingly, however, there is a recently discovered spider in Africa that can glide, sometimes jumping from tree to tree. Spiders usually eat insects and are helpful at controlling the insect population.

Science for the Ages

This is a great way to learn about spiders. For younger students, it is a great way to learn at snack time too.

Junk Drawer Plant

Make a plant model from school supplies and label the parts: stems, leaves, seeds, roots, fruits, and petals.

Biology Concept: Plant anatomy

From the Junk Drawer:

☐ School supplies   ☐ Marker
☐ Paper (or whiteboard)   ☐ Tape or glue (optional)

Step 1: Start by choosing a school supply item to represent the seed and place it near the bottom of a piece of paper (or whiteboard). Label the seed.

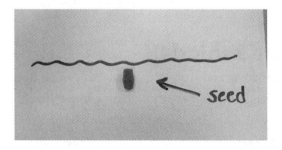

Step 2: The seed will open and grow roots downward. Pick a school supply item to represent the roots. Label the roots. From the top of the seed will grow the stem. Pick a school supply item that is straight and long to be the stem, like a pencil. Label the stem.

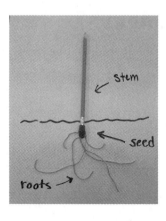

Step 3: Off the sides of the stem, leaves will form. Pick an item to represent the leaves. Put at least one on each side of the stem. Label the leaves.

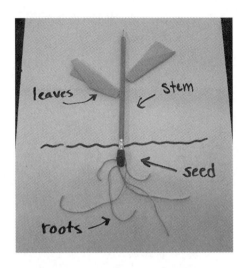

Step 4: Pick several of the same school supply item to represent the flower and its petals. Label the flower.

Step 5: You may want to also add a fruit to your plant. Pick something to represent a fruit and label it. As an option, if you're using paper instead of a whiteboard, you can tape (or glue) the school supplies in place to make a poster.

The Science Behind It

As the seed opens, roots extend down into the soil, and the stem reaches upward. Leaves grow off the stem, so the plant can get energy from the sun. Flowers soon form. The flowers are usually bright in color to attract pollinators—bees and butterflies. The pollinators help the plants spread over a larger area. Some plants will have fruit. The plant flowers first, and then a fruit grows where the flowers were. The fruit has seeds inside. Animals eat the seeds and deposit them somewhere else later.

Science for the Ages

This activity is appropriate for all ages. Encourage creativity. Models could also be made using edible things from the kitchen if homeschooling.

Little Sprout

Sprout a bean in a bag or bottle using a paper towel.

Biology Concept: Seed germination

From the Junk Drawer:

☐ Dried beans   ☐ Tape

☐ Paper towels   ☐ Window with sunlight

☐ Plastic bags

Step 1: Almost any dried beans will work for this activity, such as pinto, navy, lima, etc. Soak the beans in water overnight to speed up the process by a day or two, but you can start with completely dry beans, too. Fold a paper towel into fourths. Run it under water. You want it wet, but not dripping wet. Hold it over the sink until most of the water runs off. Put the paper towel inside a plastic bag.

Step 2: It is a good idea to use two or more beans to maximize your chances. Place the beans in the middle of the paper towel and then lightly press down on the bag around the seed to help hold the seed in place. Heavy beans (like lima beans) will fall to the bottom and that is OK. Smaller beans (like black-eyed peas) will stay in place.

Step 3: Tape the bag to a window that gets some sunlight. Keep the paper towel between the beans and the glass, so the beans can be easily observed from indoors. Avoid windows that are in the sun all the time, since this might overheat the seed. An ideal window would get at least five or six hours of sunlight a day. It is OK if the beans fall to the bottom. The lima beans pictured are heavy, so they fall. Observe the seeds over the next few days. Record the data as you see new things happening. Pay attention to what happens each day. For example, the beans split on day three, etc.

Step 5: You will eventually see roots emerge. Before they grow stems and leaves, transplant them into a pot with soil and allow them to keep growing.

The Science Behind It

Plants need sun, water, and air to grow. Soil is also important, but not critical to start the growing process. The start of the growing process is called germination. Inside every seed is a tiny plant and food to help it grow. (See the Bean Seed Dissection activity on page 87 to see what's inside a seed.)

Water is taken into the seed until the seed coat starts to split. The bean will begin to open up and send down a radicle that eventually becomes a root. The root will then send out root hairs to bring in more water. The shoot, which will later be the stem, will start to grow upward. At this point, the remnants of the seed itself are called the cotyledon. The cotyledon will eventually form the first leaves of the plant. The first leaves of the plant are small and called foliage leaves. These leaves start the photosynthesis process to provide energy for further growth. Eventually larger green leaves will grow and allow the plant to get more energy from the sun.

Science for the Ages

This is a great activity to introduce children to plant growth. For preschoolers, simply understanding what a plant needs to grow might be enough. For all ages, this can be a journal activity where students record and investigate what they see happening. A teacher can explain it, or the Internet can help them examine each step. A teacher can adapt it for older students by adding complex vocabulary. Having the students create posters is also a great way to help reinforce the concepts. All age levels can then take the plant out and place it in the soil to let it grow more. Students can also chart the growth of the sprout and the root and graph the data.

Walking Water

Create a rainbow of colors and learn a plant secret at the same time.

Biology Concepts: **Capillary action**, stems, and roots

From the Junk Drawer:

☐ Clear cups
☐ Water
☐ Food coloring
☐ Spoon (or popsicle stick)
☐ Paper towels
☐ Scissors

Step 1: Line up five clear plastic cups in a row. Fill the first, third, and fifth cup about 3/4 of the way to the top. You can also use only three cups, or more than five, as long as it is an odd number, just be sure to fill up every other cup.

Step 2: Add different colors of food coloring to the glasses that contain water. A good choice is red in the first cup, yellow in the third, and blue in the fifth. You can also experiment with different colors. Stir each glass with a spoon or popsicle stick.

Step 3: Arrange the cups so that an empty cup is between each of the colored cups of water.

Step 4: Fold a strip of paper towel in half lengthwise.

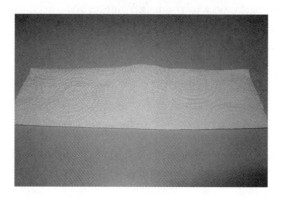

Step 5: Fold the strip again lengthwise.

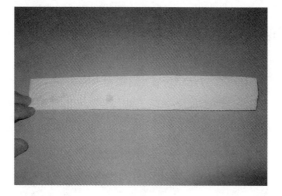

Step 6: Now, fold the strip in half, as pictured.

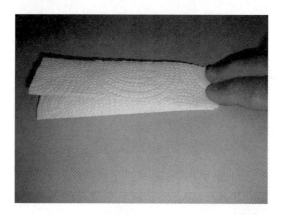

Step 7: Repeat Steps 3 through 5 until you have one fewer folded paper towels than cups. Next, stand ones of the folded paper towels next to a cup, with the fold downward. Cut length off the top (the end without the fold) so that the folded paper towel is about equal to the height of the cup. Repeat for the other folded paper towels.

Step 8: Place a folded paper towel into two cups, so that one half of it dips into a cup with colored water, and the other half rests in an empty cup. Observe what starts to happen.

Step 9: Place folded paper towels between all of the cups as shown. Let the cups sit undisturbed for at least an hour. Observe what happens periodically or come back in one hour.

Step 10: For another option, you can leave it overnight to see what happens.

The Science Behind It

Plant roots and stems use this process to pull water up into the top part of the plant. The process involves capillary action. The water will climb up the roots and stems the same way the water climbs up the paper towel. It will even "climb" down, as the activity shows. The rainbow effect is a cool side benefit of this activity.

The color mixing will let you see where certain colors come from. You should see that yellow and blue make green. Red and yellow make orange. Try experimenting with other colors if you want. What color do red and blue make?

The three colors needed to create all colors are yellow, cyan (a blue shade), and magenta (a pink shade). These are the colors used in a color printer.

Science for the Ages

This is fun and appropriate for all ages. The color mixing is a nice added benefit of this activity.

Bean Seed Dissection

Take apart a bean to learn the secrets of plants.

Biology Concepts: Parts of a seed

From the Junk Drawer:

☐ Large bean (kidney or lima bean)   ☐ Paper plate or towel

☐ Water   ☐ Magnifying glass

☐ Permanent marker   ☐ Paper and pencil (optional)

Step 1: Soak several beans for 20 to 30 minutes before you start. After they soak, you can try rubbing a bean with your fingers or using your fingernails to remove some of the bean's seed coat. This will help you visualize what the seed coat looks like, but you do not have to remove it to do the rest of the dissection. What do you think the purpose of the seed coat is?

Step 2: Now look for the tiny spot where the seed is discolored. This is easy to see on dark colored beans, like kidney beans and black-eyed peas. It is usually a small oval. This spot is called the hilum and is where the bean was originally attached to its parent plant. The hilum is a lot like your belly button. Now look for a long thin line running across the bean. Use your fingernails to separate the two halves along this line.

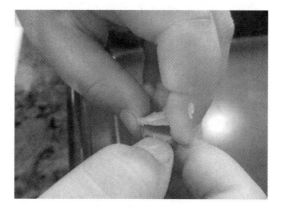

Step 3: Open up the bean and look at what you see. Most of the bean will be a large area called the cotyledon. The cotyledon is the food for the bean as it grows, until the leaves open. If you look carefully, you can find the embryo. This embryo will send a root downward and a stem upward as the plant starts to grow. An easy way to show this to other people is to use a permanent marker. Use the marker to add some color to the embryo. You may even see part of the embryo growing out of the seed halves if you are lucky.

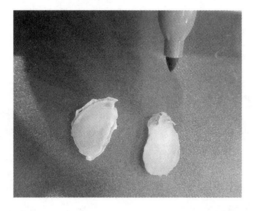

Step 4: With a magnifying glass (or just your great eyesight) you may look more carefully at the details of the beginnings of a miniature plant.

The Science Behind It

Beans are seeds. Peas, lima beans, pinto beans, and black-eyed peas are all some of the many beans you have eaten in your life. Protecting the outside of a dried bean is the seed coat. It simply protects the bean until it is planted and soaks up water. The tiny embryo will first send out a root in search of more water and nutrients from the soil. As you can see in the Little Sprout activity (page 79), the plant can grow quite large, just from the energy and nutrients already in the cotyledon. Eventually the seed coat will start being pushed up toward sunlight. When the first leaves develop, the seed coat and any remaining cotyledon will fall away.

Science for the Ages

This is perfect for all ages.

Breathing Leaf

Place a fresh leaf in water to watch the leaf breathe.
Biology Concept: **Stomata** and photosynthesis

From the Junk Drawer:

☐ Large leaf

☐ Zippered plastic bag

☐ Binder clip

☐ Water

☐ Outdoor work area

☐ Magnifying glass (optional)

Step 1: Pull a fresh leaf off an actively growing plant in the spring or summer. Make sure it is a bright, sunny day. Put the leaf inside a zippered plastic bag. Secure the stem in place using a binder clip (or clothespin).

Step 2: Fill the bag up with water. It is OK to have some air in it at this point. Seal the bag and head outside on a sunny day.

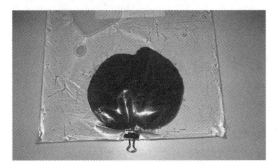

Step 3: For this step, you want an area that can get wet. Lay the bag down and open a small area in the zipper. Push out most of the air by slightly elevating the opening while the bag and leaf stay flat. If a tiny bit of air is still in the bag, that is OK. Reseal the bag.

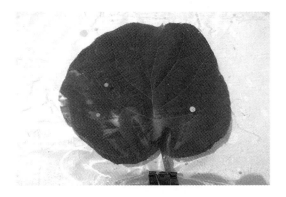

Step 4: Leave the leaf in the sunlight and watch what happens. With a magnifying glass, you might be lucky enough to see bubbles form on the leaves. After about 20 minutes, you will see oxygen bubbles inside the bag. This is oxygen that came out of the plant leaf.

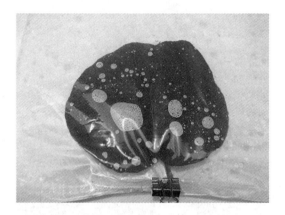

The Science Behind It

Photosynthesis is the process from which plants get their energy. The stomata (microscopic openings) in the leaves take in carbon dioxide. That carbon dioxide plus water that has come up through the roots combine to form glucose (sugar) for energy. The byproducts of this reaction are oxygen and water. Both oxygen and water come out of the stomata. Stomata are tiny openings on the surface that act almost like our mouths.

Since the bag is sealed, the oxygen bubbles you can see have been produced by the leaf as it "breathes." However, without access to new carbon dioxide, the process will eventually stop since the stomata cannot keep breathing the same carbon dioxide. The carbon dioxide that allowed the process to run was already present in the leaf when you sealed the bag, and it will be converted into the oxygen you see. Leaves are doing this every day the sun is shining. Plants have some stored glucose, so they can live while the sun is not shining.

Science for the Ages

This fun and easy activity is a great way to introduce stomata and photosynthesis. With a magnifying glass, you may even be able to see tiny bubbles on the surface of the leaves. These bubbles form right at the stomata. For middle school and high school students, it is even possible to use a microscope to see the stomata itself.

Colorful Leaves

Learn why leaves change colors in the fall.

Biology Concepts: Leaf pigment, photosynthesis, and chlorophyll

Adult supervision required

From the Junk Drawer:

- ☐ Several different types of leaves from outside
- ☐ Scissors
- ☐ Glass cups (or canning jars)
- ☐ Nail polish remover
- ☐ Marker (or wooden spoon)
- ☐ Coffee filters
- ☐ Pencil
- ☐ Rubbing alcohol
- ☐ Spoon
- ☐ Masking tape and marker (if needed for labels)

Step 1: Go outside and collect leaves from different plants and trees. You want plants and trees that lose their leaves in the winter. Keep the leaves separate from each other for best results. You can also do just one type of leaf if you choose. Write down what kinds of trees they come from if you know. You might want to ask an adult or use the computer to look up trees that are native to your area. Another great option is spinach from your salad drawer. Use the scissors to cut each leaf into tiny pieces. Put each type of leaf in its own glass cup. Canning jars also work well if you have them. Label the jars if you do more than one kind of leaf.

Step 2: Pour a tiny amount of nail polish remover in with the cut-up leaves. You only need enough to just cover the cut pieces.

Step 3: Use the blunt end of a marker or wooden spoon to grind the leaf pieces into the nail polish remover.

Step 4: Use scissors to cut a coffee filter into one-inch-wide strips. The strips need to be about one inch taller than the height of your glass cups, and you will need one strip for each leaf type. You may need more than one filter, depending on how many leaf types you try.

Step 5: Use a pencil to make a line three centimeters from the bottom of the strip. Do not use a pen or marker for this line.

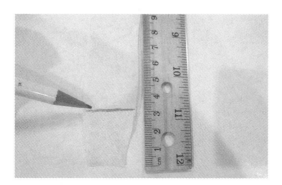

Step 6: Roll the other end of the strip around a pencil. You can adjust the length in Step 8.

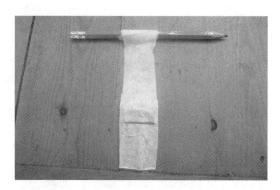

Step 7: Pour rubbing alcohol to a depth of about two centimeters in another glass cup (or jar).

Step 8: Hold the pencil next to the top of the glass cup; you want to make sure that the bottom of the strip will be long enough to reach the alcohol with the pencil line still above the alcohol.

Step 9: Take a spoon and get a little of the crushed wet leaf from the bottom of the cup.

Step 10: Place the crushed wet leaf mixture on the pencil line.

Step 11: Put the pencil over the liquid and allow the bottom of the strip to reach the alcohol. The alcohol will start to rise up the coffee filter strip. When it reaches the wet leaf mixture, the plant's pigments will dissolve in the alcohol and climb the strip.

This process is called chromatography. It will take about 20 minutes to finish the climb.

Step 12: After the liquid is no longer rising, you can take the strip out and lay it out to dry. The colors will fade a little, but you will still be able to see them. The green of the wet leaf mixture will still be visible. Above that, you will see a dark green line and more. The yellows, oranges, and reds are much lighter in color, if they are present.

The Science Behind It

Chlorophyll is the green pigment that is key to the photosynthesis process. This green pigment is very vibrant and overpowers the other pigments during the growing seasons (spring and summer). This is why the leaves are green. But leaves may contain other pigment colors. Xanthophylls are the yellow pigments, and carotenoids are the orange pigments. These pigments are also found in colored fruits and vegetables like bananas and carrots. Leaves can also contain anthocyanins, which are the reds, but plants don't produce those until autumn, if they produce them at all.

As the leaf begins to shut down for the winter, the green chlorophyll is no longer needed and breaks down. The other colors take longer to break down. As the green fades in the fall, the other pigments start to show their colors—reds, yellows, oranges, or some combination of each of these. So, in October and November, you finally get to view the beautiful colors that the leaves have had in them all along. The only exceptions are evergreen trees, which have their name for a reason. They stay green, as their chlorophyll works year-round.

Chromatography allows us to extract the pigments from the leaves. The smaller pigment molecules will climb up the paper towel the farthest. The heaviest ones are gathered near the bottom of the strip.

Science for the Ages

This activity is fun for all ages.

The long pigment names are probably best left for older students who can conduct more research. A fun research project would be to find out how early dyes and paints were made. Students could research why blue jeans are blue, and why purple is the color of royalty. Both have come about because of biology. Many dyes now are synthetic, but in the old days, dyes were derived from natural, biological sources.

Sweating Plants

Plants give off water during photosynthesis, so cover up a plant with a plastic bag to watch it breathe.

Biology Concepts: **Transpiration**, water cycle

From the Junk Drawer:

☐ Sunny day in the spring or summer
☐ Leafy plant
☐ Gallon-sized plastic bags
☐ Twist ties (or string)
☐ Medical syringe (optional)

Step 1: On a bright day, find a tree (or bush) branch that is full of green leaves. Push the branch inside a gallon-sized plastic bag. Make sure no leaves are right at the opening of the bag, then twist the open end of the bag around the branch tightly and seal with the twist ties (or string). You want a very tight seal so nothing can escape.

Step 2: Observe the bag every 15 minutes or so over the next hour. The inside of the bag will start to fog up in a very short time. You can go away and play but keep observing periodically because in time you will see even more activity.

Step 3: Gently shake the bag the next time you look at it, and you will see water run down into the bottom corner of the bag. This is the plant "sweating." The water actually comes from a process called transpiration.

Do not leave the bag on the branch for more than two hours, or you risk doing permanent damage to the leaves in the bag.

The Science Behind It

The process of water leaving leaves is called transpiration. It is very similar to humans because each time we breathe out or sweat, we lose water. Leaves lose water through tiny openings called stomata. You can think of these stomata as tiny mouths on the leaves. The stomata breathe out oxygen (see Breathing Leaf activity, page 90) and water.

A large oak tree can release over 40,000 gallons of water back into the atmosphere over the course of a year. Just another reason to love plants and trees!

Science for the Ages

This activity is appropriate for all ages. Just seeing the plants "sweat" is very eye opening, but there are several ways to modify this. You could use several bags and bag up several different types of plants. Then you could compare the amount of water given off by each. Another option is to use a different amount of leaves of the same tree and compare the amount of leaf "sweat." You could measure this in a graduated cylinder for each tree, but it would take a few minutes for the water to completely drain out of the bag. If you don't have a graduated cylinder, you can use a marked medicine syringe. Put tape over the open end and pull the plunger all the way out. Let the bag drain into the open end where the plunger came out. You can read the measurement off the markings on the syringe. You could create a bar graph depicting the number of leaves in the bag versus the amount of water obtained.

Double Up

Create a flower that's made up of two different colors.

Biology Concepts: Xylem and capillary action

From the Junk Drawer:

☐ Two cups
☐ Two colors of food coloring
☐ White flower
☐ Scissors
☐ Pipe cleaner (optional)

Step 1: Fill two cups about 2/3 full of water. Add a few drops of food coloring to one cup. Repeat for the other cup using a different color.

Step 2: Cut ¼ inch off the bottom of the flower's stem. Using scissors, split the stem of the cut flower. Once you start the cut at the bottom, you may be able to separate the stem by hand.

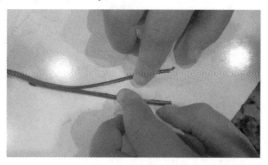

Step 3: Put one half of the stem into one glass of colored water, and the other half in the other colored water, as shown. Observe the flower over the next few hours.

If the flower has trouble standing up, you can use a pipe cleaner to give it more support. Wrap the pipe cleaner around the upper part of the stem and slide the bottom of the pipe cleaner into one of the cups.

Step 4: What does the flower look like after one day? If you don't see any change, come check each day for several days.

The Science Behind It

Normally roots carry water and nutrients via the stem to the flowers. Since you have a cut flower that no longer has its roots, the water moves directly up the stem into the flower.

All plants have tiny straw-like structures called xylem. The water is pulled up the xylem using capillary action. Capillary action will occur in any small straw-like structure.

You can also see capillary action if you dip one corner of a washcloth into the water in your sink and leave it there. If you come back in an hour, you will note that the entire washcloth will be wet. The colored water flows up the xylem all the way to a flower's petals, which is why you see the colors appear.

Science for the Ages

This is perfect for all ages. Roses and carnations seem to work the fastest (less than one day). Daisies and mums also work well. Other flowers work but may take several days. Even colored flowers work, but white shows the effect a little better. You can also use several flowers in several different cups. Each flower will have colored tips that match the various colors of water that it's absorbing.

Tap into This

Model the different types of roots using pipe cleaners.

Biology Concepts: Taproots and fibrous roots

From the Junk Drawer:

- ☐ 16 pipe cleaners (at least half light colored)
- ☐ Markers and whiteboard (or paper and pencil)
- ☐ Ruler
- ☐ Glass bowl or cup
- ☐ Food coloring
- ☐ Scissors (optional)

Step 1: Take three pipe cleaners and fold them in half. Twist the bottom together. On a whiteboard (or paper), draw the ground level and a flowering plant above it, as shown. A taproot is a single large root that goes very deep.

Step 2: For a fibrous root, take five pipe cleaners and bend them in the middle. Now bend the legs, so they go in all sorts of crazy downward directions. On the whiteboard (or paper), draw a low-lying grass plant. Fibrous roots are closer to the surface and spread out.

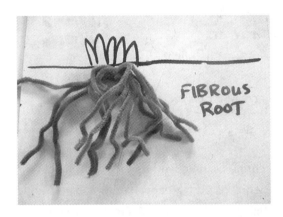

Step 3: The next few steps are so you can see how water moves up roots. These steps are best done with light-colored pipe cleaners. Fold three pipe cleaners around the center of a ruler (or pencil). Twist the bottoms together like a taproot.

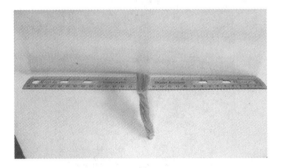

Step 4: Fill a glass bowl (or cup) halfway with water and add dark food coloring. Place the ruler across the top of the bowl. You don't want the bottom of the tap root touching the bottom, so you might need to use scissors to trim the length. Observe what happens. The dark water will start rising up the "root."

Step 5: Now take five light-colored pipe cleaners and twist them around a ruler (or pencil). To create a fibrous root, twist the pipe cleaners in different directions.

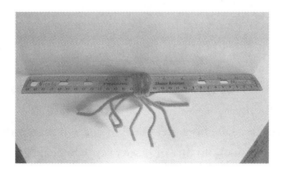

Step 6: Place the ruler across the top of the bowl and watch what happens. Again, the water will start rising up the pipe cleaner roots.

The Science Behind It

Roots serve several valuable roles for plants. They provide structure to the bottom of the plant and anchor it to the soil. They also deliver nutrients and water to the leaves and flowers; they can even store nutrients for future use.

Taproots are long, straight, deep roots. Tiny root hairs may grow off the side of the taproot, but the large central root is called the taproot. Dandelions are a common taproot plant, and many trees have taproots too. A few taproots even store large amounts of material underground, like carrots and radishes. The carrot shows you the most common shape of a taproot: a long cone shape.

Fibrous roots have many roots that are all the same size, and they grow outward underground, closer to the surface. These roots are very good for erosion control, since they take up a great deal of space underground near the surface. The many tiny roots hold dirt in place even when the ground is exposed to large amounts of water. Most grass types have a fibrous root system.

Go outside and pull up a few weeds. Not only will you surprise your parents by helping them with their yard work, but you will also be able to see what root type they have.

Science for the Ages

This activity is suitable for all ages. Older students can create more detailed models of what goes on inside the root and show all the internal parts of the root.

3

Cells and Genetics

All living things are composed of cells. The cell is the brain and powerhouse of any organism. At the smallest end of the scale are single-celled bacteria, while the most complex cellular system in the world is your own body.

Genetics is the study of how biological material is transferred from parents to offspring, whether plants or animals.

These activities will help you investigate cells and genetics, two fundamental and exciting aspects of biology.

Junk Drawer Cell Model

Build a simple model plant cell with free stuff.

Biology Concept: Plant cell modeling

From the Junk Drawer:

- ☐ Empty cereal box
- ☐ Scissors
- ☐ Marker
- ☐ Scrap paper (or sticky notes)
- ☐ Paper clips
- ☐ Hole punch

Step 1: Open an empty cereal box and pull out the plastic liner. Any thin cardboard box will do, but cereal boxes are larger and easier to write on. Cut a large back or front panel out and trim off the edge pieces. Draw two large shapes, one inside the other, that are very close together. They can be almost any shape, but do not cross the inside and outside shapes.

Label the outer line the **cell wall**. You can write on the cardboard itself or use a sticky note with an arrow pointing to the cell wall.

Label the inner line the **cell membrane**. Use the same method you used on the cell wall.

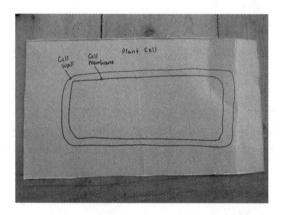

Step 2: Cut out an oval from a scrap piece of dark paper (or sticky note). Place this inside the cell membrane. This is the **nucleus**. Write the name on the oval or use a sticky note with arrows to label it.

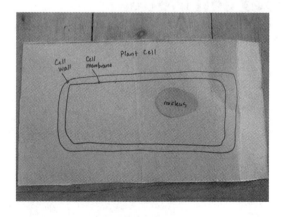

Step 3: Label the entire insides of the cell membrane with the word cytoplasm. This can also be done with a sticky note.

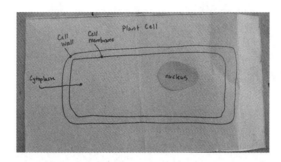

Step 4: Cut a larger oval out of a lighter piece of scrap paper (or sticky note). Label it as a vacuole.

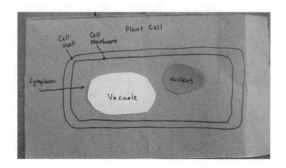

Step 5: Use large paper clips to represent **chloroplasts**. Plant cells have plenty of this organelle (a specialized part of a cell similar to an organ), so the exact number is not important. Put one down at the bottom of your model and label it, creating a key to your model.

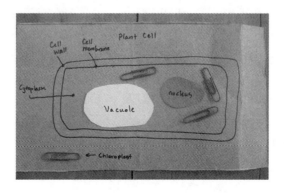

Step 6: Empty your hole punch and keep a few dots. Scatter these around inside the cell wall, but not on the nucleus or vacuole. These are the mitochondria. You can add as many as you want. Put one down at the bottom of your model and label it, adding to the key.

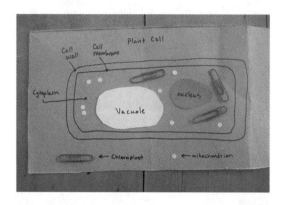

The Science Behind It

Cells that structure plants (kingdom Plantae) are called plant cells. All plant cells have some common parts. The cell wall is formed with cellulose and gives the plant strength to stand. Many animals have bones (or an exoskeleton) that gives them their strength, but plants rely on the sturdiness of their cells. The inside lining of the cell wall is called the cell membrane.

The action happens inside the cell membrane. The genetic code that is used to make new cells lives inside the nucleus. The nucleus also contains important proteins that help make new cells. The vacuole is the largest part inside the plant cell. It helps store water and all of the cell's waste products. The water inside the vacuole helps give the plant structure. The vacuole also contains necessary enzymes that help the plant grow. The chloroplasts are the fuel tanks of the plant cell. They use sunlight and water to create glucose, which helps the plant grow. The mitochondria (plural of mitochondrion) help to create the energy the cell needs. Both chloroplasts and mitochondria contain small amounts of **DNA**.

Science for the Ages

This is a simple and inexpensive way to introduce cell terms. If you create the cells with sticky notes, you can remove the names and then test yourself to see if you remember where they go. There are more organelles in a cell, but these are the major ones. As you get older, you can add more of the other organelles.

Cell models are usually built in middle school and high school life science classes. Possible alternatives are to build edible cell models with different candies or fruits or three-dimensional cell models with large foam balls and markers.

For additional practice, you can research what an animal cell looks like and build one to see the differences.

Gummy Bear Osmosis

Watch a bear grow overnight through **osmosis**.

Biology Concept: Osmosis

From the Junk Drawer:

☐ Gummy bear

☐ Cup (or any plastic container)

Step 1: Place a gummy bear in water. Leave it overnight.

Step 2: Observe the gummy bear the next day. You might want to place it next to a regular gummy bear to see the difference.

Step 3 (optional): As an additional step, you can measure your newly expanded gummy bear and a normal gummy bear. Calculate the percent change in length and width as math practice.

The Science Behind It

Osmosis is the transfer of water across the cell membrane. The skin of a gummy bear acts like a cell membrane. The water in the cup will transfer into the bear. Most sugary candies dissolve in water, but gummy bears do not. This is because they are made with gelatin, and after being cooked, the water leaves the gummy as it cools. When the bear is placed in a cup filled with water, the bear regains the water that was lost as it was cooked. In osmosis, water goes from a place with a large amount of water (outside the gummy) to an area with a lower proportion of water (inside the gummy).

Science for the Ages

This activity is appropriate for all ages. The optional Step 3 is a great math exercise for extra learning. You could try using different liquids, like salt water, sugar water, milk, vinegar, etc. You could also compare different brands of gummy bears. Keep in mind that sour gummy bears usually have a sugar coating on the outside, unlike the traditional smooth gummy bears. Would they look different at the end of this activity?

Smelly Diffusion

Learn about a cell membrane using your nose.

Biology Concepts: Osmosis, **diffusion**, and the cell membrane

From the Junk Drawer:

- [ ] Peppermint extract (or similar strong-smelling, nontoxic liquid)
- [ ] Balloon
- [ ] Empty chip can
- [ ] Syringe (optional)

Step 1: Put 10 to 15 drops of peppermint extract inside a balloon. Any strong smell like vanilla or essential oils would also work. Be careful not to get any on the outside of the balloon. You can pour it in if you are careful, or you can use an old medicine syringe if you have one.

Step 2: If you use a syringe, slide the syringe into the neck of the balloon and push down on the back. It is very important to thoroughly wash the syringe afterward.

Step 3: Tie a very tight knot in the balloon neck.

Step 4: Place the balloon inside an empty chip can and seal the lid. Let the can sit for an hour or longer.

Step 5: Open the can. Put your nose next to the open container and with your hand open, gently make circular motions toward your nose. This allows only a tiny bit of the chemical that creates the smell to enter your nose. In science classes (and the lab), this technique to smell chemicals is called wafting, and is an important technique to learn. In this experiment you are smelling something completely safe, but in the future in a science lab, you may be smelling more dangerous chemicals.

The Science Behind It

The cells in your body have a wall around them called a cell membrane. Think of it like the skin of an orange. The cell membrane lets some materials through, while stopping others.

Diffusion is when a material moves from an area of high concentration to an area of low concentration. The extract (smelly stuff) has a very high concentration inside the balloon, but a very low concentration outside of the balloon. The extract molecules will slowly move through the wall of the balloon into the can, even though the balloon is sealed. That is also the reason that a filled party balloon will eventually deflate on its own, even if you don't pop it.

The type of materials in the wall makes a difference regarding the rate of diffusion. For example, shiny metallic Mylar balloons may take several weeks to deflate, whereas regular latex balloons will deflate in one or two days.

Osmosis is a very special type of diffusion. Osmosis is the process of water moving through a membrane. Water moves in and out of your cells using osmosis. You can see osmosis at work in the next two activites, as well.

Science for the Ages

This activity is suitable for all ages. It is a great way to introduce the cell membrane. It is also a great classroom experiment. One chip can can be used for the entire class as it can be passed around. You could also keep a Mylar balloon and a latex balloon for a few days to watch what happens. This is a great way to "recycle" party balloons into learning tools.

The Incredible Growing Glow-in-the-Dark Egg

Make an egg grow using diffusion.

Biology Concepts: Diffusion, cell membrane, and hypotonic solutions

From the Junk Drawer:

☐ Egg

☐ Glass

☐ Vinegar

☐ Ruler

☐ Cell phone or camera

☐ Fork or toothpick

☐ Old highlighter (optional)

☐ Pliers (optional)

☐ Black light (UV) flashlight (optional)

Step 1: First, dissolve the shell on an egg. Place an egg in a glass and cover it in vinegar, then let it sit for 24 hours. This will dissolve the calcium and leave the egg enclosed by the cell membrane.

Step 2: Take out the egg and rinse it off. You can gently bounce it on the counter (or just lightly squeeze it) to see the rubber egg in action.

Step 3 (optional): Place a ruler next to the egg and take a picture of it. The egg is bigger than it was before because it has absorbed water from the vinegar. The egg has grown because of osmosis. For more fun, do Steps 4, 5, and 6. Or skip ahead to Step 7.

Step 4 (optional): Take the top off an old highlighter. Next, remove the writing wick of the highlighter. You will probably need pliers to do this.

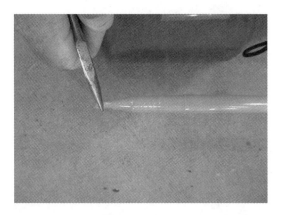

Step 5 (optional): Rinse out the glass and place the rubber egg back inside it. Fill the cup with water. Place the writing wick in the water with the egg and let it sit for 24 hours.

Step 6 (optional): Pull the egg out and play with it. If you took a picture before, compare the new size to the old size. If you did optional Steps 4 and 5, turn off the lights and look at the egg with a black light (UV) flashlight. It will glow! (The picture shows the UV flashlight but not the egg glowing in the dark, as the glow is hard to capture with a camera.)

Step 7: Once you are done playing with the egg, place it in the sink. Use a fork or toothpick to pierce the skin of the egg. The flexible sac on the egg is the cell membrane of the egg. Wash your hands thoroughly after doing this.

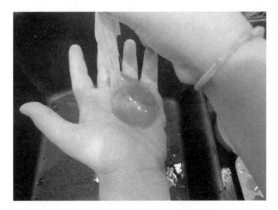

The Science Behind It

Once the eggshell is dissolved, the cell membrane holds the egg together. This membrane is a **semipermeable membrane**. That means it allows certain molecules through and stops others. Almost all cells need water, so water can cross this membrane easily.

The glass filled with water in this experiment is a hypotonic solution. That means it has a greater amount of water per volume than is found inside the egg. Therefore, water flows into the egg, and the egg grows. This is another example of osmosis, the movement of water through a membrane.

Science for the Ages

This activity is great for all ages. It is very important to wash your hands well after doing this activity. If you're older, you could find the mass of the rubber egg before and after soaking in the liquid. This would allow you to calculate the percentage of weight gained. With some additional chemistry, you could even calculate the number of water molecules that passed through the membrane.

The Incredible Shrinking Glow-in-the-Dark Egg

Make a glow-in-the-dark egg with a sugar solution using highlighters and vinegar-soaked eggs.

Biology Concepts: Diffusion, cell membrane, and hypertonic solutions

From the Junk Drawer:

☐ Egg
☐ Glass
☐ Vinegar
☐ Ruler
☐ Cell phone or camera

☐ Light corn syrup (or salt water)
☐ Spoon
☐ Old highlighter (optional)
☐ Pliers (optional)
☐ Black light (UV) flashlight (optional)

Step 1: First, dissolve the shell on an egg. Place an egg in in a glass and cover it in vinegar, then let it sit for 24 hours. This will dissolve the calcium and leave the egg enclosed by the cell membrane.

Step 2: Take out the egg and rinse it off. You can gently bounce it on the counter (or just lightly squeeze it) to see the rubber egg in action.

Step 3 (optional): Place a ruler next to the egg and take a picture of it.

Step 4: Rinse out the glass. Pour light corn syrup into the glass until the egg is completely submerged. Get an adult's permission to do this beforehand because of the cost and mess. Watch the egg for the next few hours. You can also do it with salt dissolved in water. The egg won't shrink as much, but it will still shrink and may not be as messy.

Step 5: Place a heavy spoon on top of the egg to keep the egg beneath the surface. It will still work without the spoon, but the exposed part of the egg will harden, and the egg will not keep its oval shape. For more fun, do Steps 6 and 7. Or skip ahead to Step 8.

Step 6 (optional): Take the top off an old highlighter. Next, remove the writing wick of the highlighter. You will probably need pliers to do this.

Step 7 (optional): Rinse out the glass and place the rubber egg back inside it. Fill the cup with water. Place the writing wick in the water with the egg and let it sit for 24 hours.

Step 8: Pull out the egg and rinse it off. You can push it now to see how soft (or hard) it is. If you took a picture before, compare the new size to the old size. The egg has shrunk because of osmosis.

If you did the optional Steps 6 and 7, turn off the lights and look at the egg with a black light (UV) flashlight. It will glow!

You can return it back to its normal size by putting it back in tap water for about one hour. Dispose of the egg and wash your hands thoroughly when done.

The Science Behind It

The eggshell dissolves off the egg because the acetic acid in the vinegar dissolves the calcium carbonate of the eggshell. You probably saw the bubbles forming on the egg as this happened. That is the carbon dioxide that is given off in the reaction. The calcium remains in the water.

The rubber egg is held together by the cell membrane. This cell membrane is semipermeable. That means it only allows certain molecules to get through. Water is necessary for our cells, so it travels back and forth through the cell membrane by a process called osmosis.

The corn syrup (or salt water) is a hypertonic solution. That means it contains more solute (salt or sugar) than water. In fact, it contains less water than the egg cell. Because of this, water will flow across the cell membrane out of the egg, causing the egg to shrink. This is the major reason why it's important not to drink the ocean's salt water. It actually dehydrates (removes water from) your body. You think you're drinking water, but the salt pulls water out of your cells, which is not good.

Science for the Ages

This is safe for all ages. It is very important to wash your hands well after doing this activity. The corn syrup works faster and provides a more dramatic effect than the salt water, but it costs more and is messier. If you're older, you could find the mass of the rubber egg before and after soaking the egg in the liquid. This would allow you to calculate the percentage of weight lost. With some additional chemistry, you could even calculate the number of water molecules that passed through the membrane.

Play-Doh Mitosis

Model how a cell divides during **mitosis** with Play-Doh.

Biology Concept: Mitosis

From the Junk Drawer:

- ☐ Play-doh (2 colors)
- ☐ Paper plates
- ☐ Glue
- ☐ Sticky notes
- ☐ Marker
- ☐ Stapler

Step 1: Create two large Xs out of different colors of Play-Doh. Place the Xs on a paper plate in a random pattern. Glue the Xs in place. This is the first step in cell division, and it is called **prophase.** The Xs that are being created are chromosomes. During this process, DNA duplicates itself. Write "prophase" on a sticky note and attach it lightly to the paper plate.

Step 2: Create two large Xs again out of the same colors as the previous Xs. Place one X near the top and the other near the bottom of another plate. Use a marker to draw lines as shown. The second phase is called **metaphase**. During this phase, the DNA (chromosomes) lines up in the middle of the cell. The DNA starts to get pulled to the sides of the cell. Write "metaphase" on a sticky note and lightly attach it to the plate.

Step 3: Now the chromosomes split. On another plate, use a marker to draw lines pulling the split chromosomes further to each side as shown. Create two small Vs of each color. Place the Vs along the marker lines toward the sides of the cell. This phase is called **anaphase**. Write "anaphase" on a sticky note and lightly attach it to the plate.

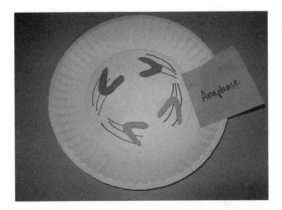

Step 4: Now the new cells start to separate. On another plate, draw two circles to represent the cell membrane for each new cell. Create two lines each of the same colors as before. These lines represent the chromosomes. Glue one chromosome of each color inside each circle. This represents **telophase**, where the cell division nears completion. Write "telophase" on a sticky note and lightly attach it to the plate.

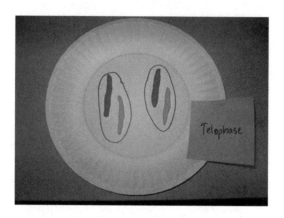

Step 5: Now create two separate new cells on different plates. Glue two chromosome lines, one of each color, inside each cell. This phase is called **cytokinesis**. You have now created two new cells called daughter cells. Mitosis is complete, and the new cells are ready to divide again if needed. Write "cytokinesis" on a sticky note and lightly attach it to one of the plates.

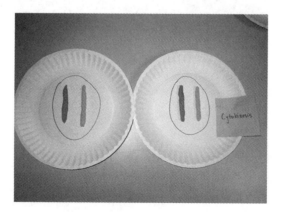

Step 6: After the glue dries, staple the paper plates together with the prophase model going first. You probably need to staple once from each side for the best hold. Attach metaphase to prophase, anaphase to metaphase, and so on.

Step 7: Put the two daughter cells side by side and staple them to the bottom of the first four plates. You can now pull off the sticky notes and practice putting them back in the correct place.

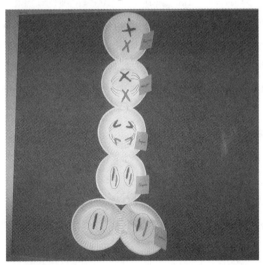

The Science Behind It

Mitosis is the process that creates new cells in living organisms. Each daughter cell is an exact duplicate of its parent cell. We grow new cells for our skin, muscles, and all of our organs in this manner. Plants also use this to create new plant cells. Mitosis is the primary way of making new cells. This means that, when your cells wear out, mitosis helps your body replace them.

Mitosis is a type of asexual reproduction because the new cell is an exact duplicate of the original cell. Mitosis is primarily used for growth and repair of the cells in your body. The parent cell has 46 chromosomes, and each daughter cell also has 46 chromosomes. This is a little different from meiosis, which is described in the next activity.

Science for the Ages

This activity is appropriate for elementary age and up. Trying to place the sticky notes where they belong is a great way to practice getting the steps in order. Teachers could even make it an entrance ticket to class if they wanted. Upper level students could add more detail and label additional parts like centrioles, centromeres, chromosomes, and tubules. This could also be done on one paper plate, simply moving the Play-Doh to show the different phases. The hands-on component will help students memorize the phases.

Play-Doh Meiosis

Model the steps of **meiosis** with Play-Doh.

Biology Concepts: Meiosis and sexual reproduction

From the Junk Drawer:

☐ Paper plates
☐ Play-doh (2 colors)
☐ Sticky notes

☐ Marker
☐ Small paper plates (or scissors)

Step 1: Meiosis is made up of two different parts, commonly called meiosis I and meiosis II. A cell normally exists in a state called **interphase**, which literally means "between phases." Interphase is the common state of the cells before meiosis starts.

The first phase of meiosis I is called prophase I. During prophase I, the chromosomes pair up, starting to form a feature that's actually large enough to be seen under a high-powered microscope.

On a paper plate, create four Xs out of Play-Doh to represent the chromosomes. Label this phase and each following as you create them so you can quiz yourself later—sticky notes and a marker work well for this.

Step 2: Also during prophase I, a process called crossing over occurs. This is when the chromosomes swap some DNA. To show crossing over, move a little DNA (Play-Doh) from one chromosome to another.

Step 3: In metaphase I, the chromosomes line up in the center of the cell. The chromosomes start to get pulled to the edges. Use a marker to draw lines pulling the chromosomes to opposite sides of the cell.

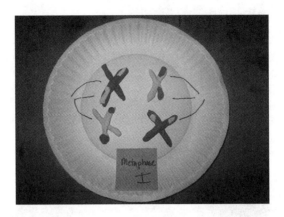

Step 4: In anaphase I, the chromosomes start to separate into chromatids (individual parts of the X). Pull apart the parts of your chromosomes and place them on the edges of the paper plate.

Step 5: In telophase I, the chromatids recombine, and two new cells start to form. Form the individual chromatids back into Xs. They can come back together in any combination, which leads to genetic differences. Use a new plate and draw circles (or dotted circles) around the new cells.

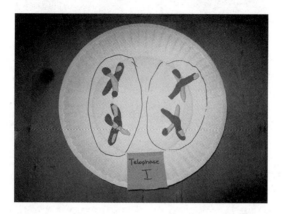

Step 6: For the following steps, you can use small paper plates, or you can use scissors to cut out the small, flat bottoms of large paper plates.

Step 7: For prophase II, put two chromosomes each on two of the smaller plates. These two cells are called daughter cells, since they each contain DNA from both parents.

Step 8: In metaphase II, the chromosomes line up in the middle. Move your Play-Doh chromosomes to the middle of each cell.

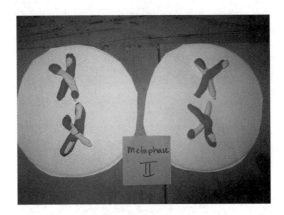

Step 9: During anaphase II, the chromosomes split. Pull the individual pieces of the chromosomes apart and move them to the edges of the daughter cells.

Step 10: In telophase II, new cells start to form. You can straighten the Play-Doh chromatids and draw circles around them.

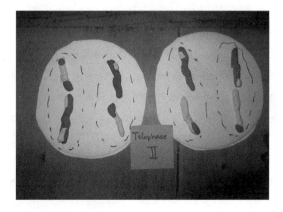

Step 11: Cut four smaller shapes and place the chromosomes from the daughter cells onto these four new cells. Meiosis is now complete. The final cell division is called cytokinesis. These are often referred to as granddaughter cells.

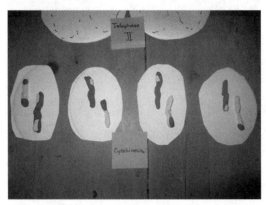

The Science Behind It

Each parent cell has 46 chromosomes. Meiosis creates sets of cells that have 23 chromosomes. The cells in the first set are called daughter cells, and the process of forming them is called meiosis I. These daughter cells each split into four granddaughter cells, each containing 23 chromosomes. The genetic material is slightly different in each granddaughter cell.

Meiosis is a process that creates new living beings. It is a type of sexual reproduction that happens in plants and animals. Meiosis is the reason that two sisters can look different, even if they have the same parents. It is important because it adds genetic diversity. The granddaughter cells are called gametes. In animals, these are the sperm and the eggs. In plants, they are called gametophytes.

In conclusion, mitosis (see previous activity) creates new cells that are the same as the parent cell. Meiosis creates new cells that are completely different from the parent cell and that combine with other cells to create new life.

Science for the Ages

This activity is suitable for all ages above early elementary. Playing with the Play-Doh is fun and helps to emphasize the crossing over of genetic material. This could also be done (like the mitosis activity) with glue. The daughter cells and granddaughter cells could also be done with small paper plates instead of the circles cut out of the bigger plates. Using sticky notes to label the phases is a great way to practice putting the steps in order, even after you are done building new cells.

Pipe Cleaner Nerves

Build a **neuron** with pipe cleaners.

Biology Concepts: Nerves and nerve conduction

From the Junk Drawer:

☐ Pipe cleaners (5 different colors) ☐ Marker or pencil
☐ Paper ☐ Scissors

Step 1: Ball up one pipe cleaner. You will be adding things to the ball, so you don't want it super tight. This will represent the cell body. You can place it on a piece of paper and label it now, or you can build the entire nerve cell before you label the pieces.

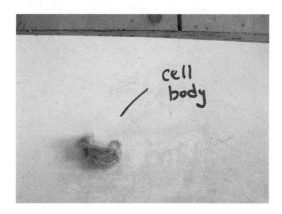

Step 2: Take a long pipe cleaner of a different color and fold it in half. Slide both ends through the cell body and twist the two pieces together. This represents the axon.

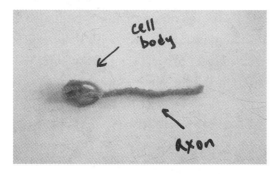

Step 3: Cut another differently colored pipe cleaner into four or five pieces. Push these into the cell body on the side opposite the axon. Twist them at all different angles as shown. These are the dendrites.

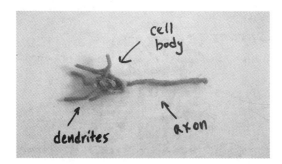

Step 4: Twist a pipe cleaner of a fourth color around the axon. It would work best to have this pipe cleaner be a different color than the one used for the axon, so that it can be clearly seen. This is called the myelin sheath. Trim the end with scissors if you have too much left.

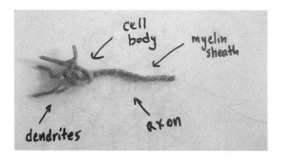

Step 5: Wrap 1/2 of another pipe cleaner of a different color around the end of the axon (opposite of the cell body). This represents the synaptic terminal. Lay your nerve on a piece of paper and label all the parts if you didn't label them as you worked.

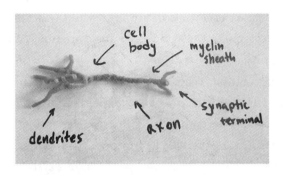

Step 6: If you make more than one model, you can line them up. This chain of nerves helps show what happens when your body sends a message to your brain or when your brain sends a message to your body. The message gets picked up by the dendrites, then sent down the axon to the dendrites of another nerve cell, and then the message travels through the next nerve in the same way, and this continues until it reaches its destination in the body.

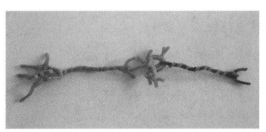

The Science Behind It

"Nerve" is a simple name for a neuron. A neuron is the type of cell that carries electrical signals throughout your body. If you want to make a fist, neurons carry electrical signals from your brain to your forearm. The signal goes down your spinal cord, then down your arm until it reaches your forearm. The forearm muscles contract, pulling your fingers into a fist. This is all done with one long chain of neurons.

A neuron is just another type of cell in your body, complete with genes and all the other cell parts. But it has a few parts that help it send the messages. The dendrites are special parts that bring the message into the cell body. The axon is the part that sends messages to another neuron. Putting this together with your brain can give you a picture of your nervous system. This system controls your muscles and much more.

Your feet get cold because they send a signal to your brain along these neurons. Smells travel from your nose to your brain along a series of these neurons. When you eat a jalapeño pepper, a signal communicating heat makes its way to your brain. Neurons are very important. They even work while you are asleep to keep your heart and lung muscles working.

Science for the Ages

This project is easy for all ages. Even preschoolers would have fun making the neurons. Older students could label the parts, define the functions, and turn in their diagrams. Let them go home with their modeled nerve cells to create conversation. You can also unwind the pipe cleaners and keep for future projects.

Candy DNA

Create an edible DNA model. Learn the shape and structure of DNA.

Biology Concepts: DNA structure and parts

From the Junk Drawer:

☐ Gumdrops (4 colors)
☐ Paper towels
☐ Marker
☐ Toothpicks
☐ Licorice ropes
☐ Kitchen shears (optional)

Step 1: Divide the gumdrops into four different colored piles on a paper towel. Gummy bears and any soft candy will work. Label the piles A, G, T, and C. The letters represent adenine, guanine, thymine, and cytosine, the four nitrogen bases in DNA.

Step 2: Push a candy from the A pile onto one end of a toothpick. Be careful with the pointed end. Push a candy from the T pile onto the other end of the same toothpick. Leave a small gap between the two candies. Adenine and thymine always go on the same toothpick, just like in real DNA. Guanine and cytosine will always pair up also. Repeat until you have at least five toothpicks full. Any combination of A-T and G-C toothpicks is fine.

Step 3: Push one end of the toothpick through a licorice rope candy. Again, be careful with the sharp ends of the toothpicks. The rope candy represents the sugar-phosphate backbone that holds the base pairs together. Push the other end through another piece of licorice rope candy.

Step 4: Repeat for the remaining four or five toothpicks. The order doesn't matter, and which nitrogen bases are on each side also doesn't matter. Real DNA strands are long and random, which makes all DNA different for different people, plants, and animals.

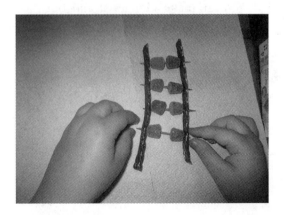

Step 5: DNA forms a double helix shape. It looks like a twisted ladder. You can create this effect in two ways. You can either twist the rope candy on both ends with your hands or, as an easier alternative, pinch the middle of the bottom and top toothpicks and twist them in opposite directions.

After you have finished, show your DNA strand off to a friend or your parents. You can make it longer in the next few steps if you want. You can also skip to Step 9 to see how DNA comes apart.

Step 6 (optional): You can make a longer strand, but you may need adult help. Repeat Steps 1 through 5 to create a second DNA set. Push toothpicks into both licorice ropes at one end of the new DNA strand.

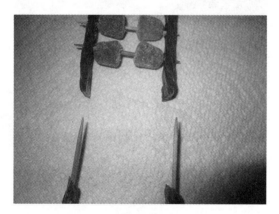

Step 7 (optional): Push the other end of the toothpicks into the licorice ropes of the other DNA set. Slowly slide each side a little at a time until the rope candies meet.

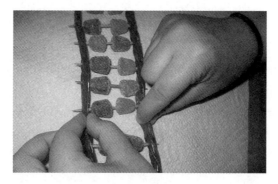

Step 8: Twist the longer strand just as in Step 6.

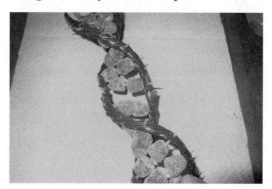

Step 9 (optional): To show how DNA comes apart in reproduction, you can cut the toothpicks with a pair of kitchen shears (if you have permission). The parts will then recombine into new DNA.

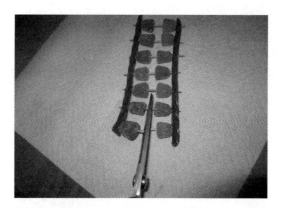

The Science Behind It

DNA, which stands for deoxyribonucleic acid, is the fundamental building material of all living things. DNA is a long chain of material that contains our genetic code. It is a set of instructions on how to create all of the proteins we need to survive.

DNA is shaped like a double helix, a twisted ladder shape. It is composed of four base building blocks: adenine, cytosine, guanine, and thymine. These are held together by hydrogen bonds. Your DNA is copied through mitosis as you grow. DNA can also be combined with another living being's DNA to form a baby during meiosis.

Science for the Ages

Building the candy DNA is appropriate for all ages. Naming the individual parts is probably for elementary age and above. This is a great introduction activity to mitosis and meiosis for older students.

DNA Extraction

See DNA without a microscope

Biology Concepts: DNA

Adult supervision required

From the Junk Drawer:

- ☐ Cold rubbing alcohol
- ☐ Banana (or strawberry or kiwi)
- ☐ Resealable plastic bag
- ☐ Measuring cups
- ☐ Salt
- ☐ 2 clear glasses
- ☐ Liquid dish detergent
- ☐ Strainer (or funnel and coffee filter)
- ☐ Spoon
- ☐ Toothpick (or skewer or tweezers)

Step 1: Put a bottle of rubbing alcohol in the freezer because you will need it to be cold later. Place a piece of banana, strawberry, or kiwi in the resealable plastic bag and squeeze out as much air as possible. Seal the bag.

Step 2: Squish the fruit with your fingers. You want it to be almost liquid.

Step 3: Add 1/2 teaspoon of salt to 1/2 cup of water in a glass. Stir the salt to get it to dissolve.

Step 4: Add two teaspoons of liquid dish detergent to the cup. Mix gently to avoid making bubbles.

Step 5: Add about 1/4 of the salt, detergent, and water mix to the resealable baggie. Squish out as much air as possible. Knead the bag with your fingers to mix it up some more. Lay the baggie flat and let it sit for 20 minutes.

Step 6: After 20 minutes, filter out the plant material. Place a kitchen strainer over a small clear glass. You can also use a funnel with a coffee filter. Use the back of a spoon to extract more liquid, but don't break the filter.

Step 7: DNA is soluble in water, so you will use cold rubbing alcohol to help get the DNA out. Slightly tilt the glass. Gently pour one teaspoon of alcohol down the side of the glass. The alcohol will float on the banana juice.

Step 8: If you keep an eye on it, you will see the DNA appear. It will be a white solid between the alcohol and banana mixture.

Step 9: Use a toothpick (or skewer or tweezers) to remove some of the DNA. You can store the DNA in a small bottle if you put it in alcohol. If you leave the glass jar alone, more DNA will appear.

The Science Behind It

Deoxyribonucleic acid is better known as DNA. DNA is the fundamental building block of **genes** that make all living organisms. The individual DNA strands look like a twisted ladder, but they are far too tiny to see. Smashing the fruit breaks open the cells and allows the DNA to escape. But the DNA is soluble in water, so you need the alcohol to pull it out.

Science for the Ages

This activity will require an adult's help at least until middle school, but should be fine for that age and above. You could extend this by trying different fruits. You could also play with the exact amount of dish detergent and salt, but sometimes you might get no results. A teacher I know buys little necklace containers for the students, so they can wear the DNA they extract.

Cereal Proteins

Learn the secret to **RNA** with edible treats.

Biology Concepts: Proteins, DNA, RNA, **transcription**

From the Junk Drawer:

- ☐ Multicolored ring cereal (like Fruit Loops)
- ☐ Pipe cleaners
- ☐ Tape
- ☐ Paper (or sticky notes)
- ☐ Pencil
- ☐ Cups

Step 1: Slide 8 to 10 pieces of colorful cereal rings onto a pipe cleaner. The colors can be completely random. Curl the ends so the cereal pieces stay in place. This construction represents DNA in the nucleus, which gives the cell instructions on how to make a protein. Tape the DNA in place, so it can't move. Place paper (or a sticky note) and pencil next to the protein.

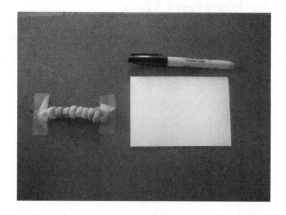

Step 2: Copy the color pattern onto a piece of paper. For example, if you have red, yellow, red, green, red, yellow, red, and green, record that as RYRGRYRG. This code represents RNA, which, like DNA, is a nucleic acid. It provides the protein code for the cell. When you copy the code, you are engaging in a process called transcription.

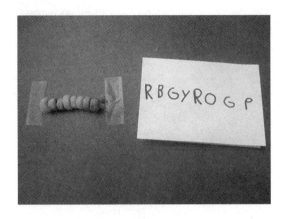

Step 3: Take a cupful of cereal, your paper code, and a few pipe cleaners to another room. Build the same protein, using your transcription as a guide. Repeat the process by going to yet another room with your cup and pipe cleaners. Assembling the proteins represents **translation**, where you make copies of the original protein.

Step 4: Bring your proteins back and compare them to the original protein. Are they the same or different? Most likely they will be the same, but they might be different, if you mixed something up. In real cells, sometimes a mistake is made in transcription or translation. This results in a slightly different protein.

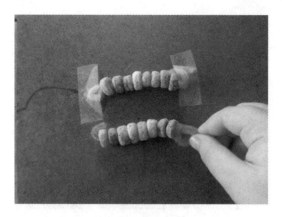

The Science Behind It

The nucleus of the cell contains DNA, which is the template for the formation of proteins. The different colors represent the amino acids that make up proteins. When you copy the order of the proteins, this is called transcription. Transcription is the process that moves the pattern of amino acids out of the nucleus. The movable paper code in this activity represents RNA. Making a new protein from the RNA code is called translation. The original DNA never leaves the nucleus, but transcription and translation allow your body to make copies of the protein outside of the nucleus, using the code found in the DNA.

Science for the Ages

This activity is suitable for elementary age and up and is great for the class-room. Put one DNA template in the corner and move cups of cereal and pipe cleaners throughout the room. Each student can make his or her own protein and compare it to the original. Imperfect copies are a great way to show that mistakes happen, even in the human body.

Paper Clip Punnett Square

Create a **Punnett square** using paper clips.

Biology Concepts: Punnett squares, homozygous and heterozygous **alleles**

From the Junk Drawer:

☐ Large and small paper clips
☐ Whiteboard and markers (or pen and paper)

Step 1: Review some useful vocabulary terms before you start this activity. A **trait** is what shows up in a living organism, like eye color for people or flower color for plants. A **dominant gene** is one that shows up over a **recessive gene**. Homozygous means both genes are the same, and heterozygous means both genes are different. A combination of the genes is called an allele. After combining alleles from two parents, the cross is called a genotype. The trait that shows up in the offspring (such as brown eyes) as a result of its unique genotype is the **phenotype**.

A Punnett square is a way of showing how alleles can possibly combine to then be expressed as traits.

Step 2: Large paper clips represent dominant genes, and small paper clips represent recessive genes. This activity demonstrates the different possible combinations of alleles. A homozygous dominant allele has two dominant genes and is shown by two large paper clips. A homozygous recessive allele has two recessive genes and is shown by two small paper clips. Finally, a heterozygous allele has one large and one small paper clip to represent one dominant and one recessive gene.

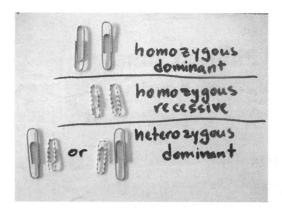

Step 3: Draw a box on a whiteboard (or piece of paper) and then further divide it into four squares as shown. In this step, you are going to cross a homozygous dominant genotype (two large paper clips) with a heterozygous genotype (One large and one small paper clip).

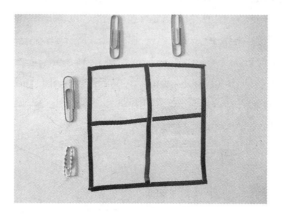

Step 4: In the top left square, you want to place the two types of paper clips that intersect there: a large (dominant) paper clip from the top and a large (dominant) paper clip from the side; the box will end up having two large paper clips (homozygous dominant genotype).

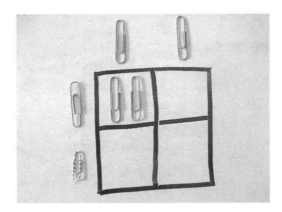

Step 5: The top right square should also contain two large (dominant) paper clips.

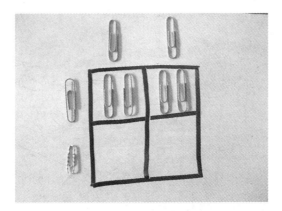

Step 6: The lower left box is completed with one large paper clip and one small (recessive) paper clip. This represents a heterozygous dominant genotype.

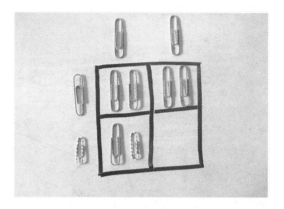

Step 7: The remaining square is also completed with one large and one small paper clip. Your finished Punnett square has four squares that each contain a dominant gene. That means all of the offspring in this arrangement would express the dominant trait.

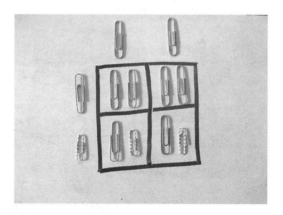

Step 8: Move the paper clips and try the combination shown below. This represents two heterozygous dominant alleles combining.

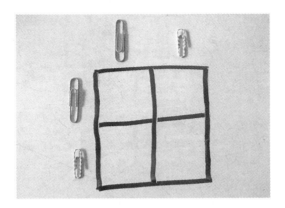

Step 9: This is what your finished Punnett square will look like. Three out of the four squares have a dominant gene, so three fourths (or 75 percent) of the possible genotypes will express the dominant gene. On average, one fourth of the offspring will express the recessive gene.

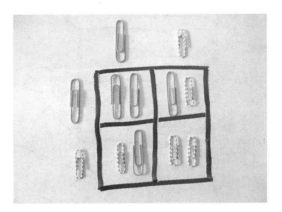

Step 10: Now try this Punnett square. This represents a homozygous dominant allele being crossed with a homozygous recessive allele.

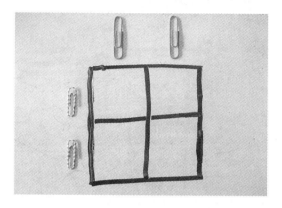

Step 11: The finished square should look like this. All four squares contain a dominant gene, so all of the offspring would express the dominant trait.

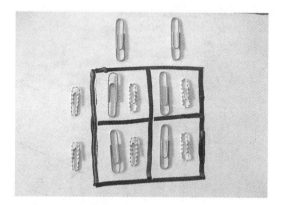

Step 12: Punnett squares are usually completed with letters as shown; the capital letters represent dominant genes and the lowercase letters represent recessive genes. Draw this one and try it. Simply fill in the letters the same way you filled in the paper clips.

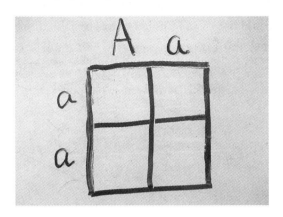

Step 13: This is the finished square using letters. Exactly half of the offspring would express the dominant trait, and half would express the recessive trait.

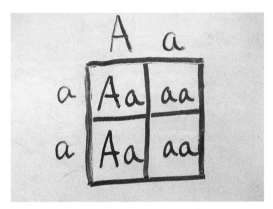

The Science Behind It

Punnett squares are used to predict the genotypes when two parents have offspring. The top of the square represents the allele of one parent. The side of the square represents the allele of the other parent. Dominant genes and their corresponding traits (like brown eye color) are more likely to be expressed. That is the reason why so many people have brown eyes.

Science for the Ages

This is a great introduction to Punnett squares and the vocabulary associated with them. Paper clips are readily available and reusable, so they make for perfect lab equipment. You could also substitute binder clips or large and small sticky notes. You could use colored poker chips, but the different sizes help students remember dominant better. The large and small sizes help students remember the terms dominant and recessive. In a classroom setting, it is easy to walk around and monitor this activity as it happens.

4

Biology Tools

All branches of science have tools scientists use to learn and study. Biologists use magnifying glasses and microscopes to see the small things around them. Other tools will help you learn about how biology works. Here are a few biology tools you can build that cost next to nothing.

Classification Cards

Learn how to classify living things.

Biology Concept: Classification of living things

From the Junk Drawer:

☐ Index cards
☐ Marker
☐ Scissors

Step 1: Fold an index card in half, making a tent. Any size of index card will work. This could also be done with scrap paper from the recycling bin.

Write a capital K on one side of the tent. Write the word "Kingdom" on the other side.

Step 2: Fold another card in half and cut about ¼ of an inch off the bottom, so that it makes a shorter tent. Write a capital P on one side of the tent. Write the word "Phylum" on the other side.

Step 3: Repeat Step 2 with five additional cards, making each card a little shorter than the previous card. Write the capital letter on one side and the name on the other side. The correct order, following K and P, will be C ("Class"), O ("Order"), F ("Family"), G ("Genus"), and S ("Species"). When finished, slide the edge of each card into its larger counterpart, as shown. This represents how biologists classify living things.

Step 4: If you turn the cards around you can see the names of the classification system components in order.

Step 5: The cards can be slid together and held with a paperclip for a later study session.

The Science Behind It

The classification system for living things was first written about by Carl Linnaeus in 1735. He devised a system that made sure every organism could be classified. Now, scientists classify living things using six different kingdoms, or eight, depending on who you ask. The exact number is continuously debated, as life and the study of it are ever-changing.

The two kingdoms we explore in this book are plants (Plantae) and animals (Animalia). Kingdom Animalia includes all animals. As you move down the classification list, the types of animals included in each classification narrows. Phylum is the second layer, then class, order, family, genus, and species. The species will tell you the exact name of the animal you are studying.

Science for the Ages

This is perfect for elementary students and above. Older students could classify actual living things with their Latin names. A teacher (or parent, or student) could look up and print the classification for a living organism. You could then cut out the names and place them in the correct order according to the classification. You could also write the names of the six major kingdoms inside the first card.

Dichotomous School Supplies

Make your own dichotomous key from items found in your book bag

Biology Concept: Dichotomous key

From the Junk Drawer:

☐ School supplies (pencils, pens, crayons, colored pencils, erasers. rulers, etc.)

☐ Whiteboard and markers (or a large piece of paper and markers)

☐ Computer with Internet access (optional)

Step 1: Lay out all of your school supplies in front of you. It helps to do this on a whiteboard or large piece of paper.

What is one question that could be answered with either a yes or a no that would divide your supplies? For example, does the item write?

Draw arrows as shown leading to each answer.

Step 2: Put all the items that write under *yes* and the items that do not under *no*. Think of another question that could be answered with a yes or a no, now concerning only the writing tools.

Step 3: One example of a good question is: will the writing be permanent? Separate the writing supplies that leave permanent marks from the supplies that leave marks you can erase. Think of another question that concerns only the permanent writing supplies.

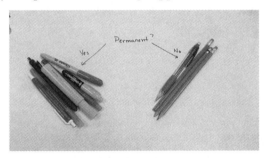

Step 4: For example, do the writing tools have a fine tip? Separate the items based on that question. Think of another question that concerns only the fine-tipped writing tools. It is OK if you run out of questions.

Step 5: Look at the school supplies that do not write and think of a question that could separate them into two groups. A good question might be: does the school supply erase pencil marks? Separate the supplies into erasers and non-erasers.

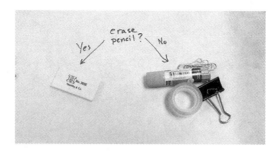

Step 6: Now think of a question that will further divide the pile of non-erasers. A good question might be: is it sticky?

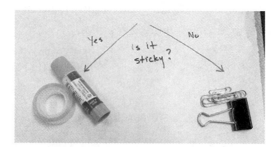

Step 7: Keep separating things until each school supply is left by itself or with a very small, specific group. Your key will look different from the one pictured if you started with different supplies or asked different questions.

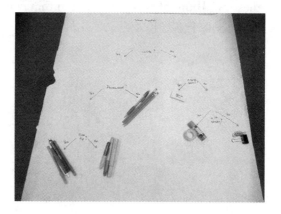

Step 8: To help other people use your dichotomous key, go back and list the different supplies you started with. You can also list the questions you used to separate the items.

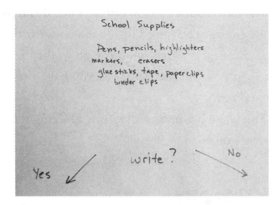

Step 9: Most of the time you will use a dichotomous key that has already been created by someone else. A common example is a tree (or leaf) identification key. With parents' permission, search online for a dichotomous key for tree identification. Go outside and pull a leaf off a tree. Use the key to identify the type of tree the leaf came from.

The Science Behind It

Dichotomous keys are commonly used in the study of life. They are used to identify reptiles, trees, leaves, and more. Dichotomous means "having two parts." The keys allow you to identify almost any living thing, using a series of yes-or-no questions. The questions are based on some observable trait.

For example, let's look at the study of vertebrates. These are animals that have an internal skeleton. The first question is, does it have fur? If the answer is yes, the animal is a mammal. If the answer is no, you move on to the next question: does the animals have feathers? If yes, it is a bird. If no, you move on to the next question: are the eggs fertilized inside the body? If the answer is yes, you have a reptile. If the answer is no, you move on to the next question: does the adult animal have gills? If the answer is yes, you have a fish. If the answer is no, you have an amphibian.

Dichotomous keys are a big part of the study of living things. And now you know how to create one.

Science for the Ages

This activity is appropriate for elementary age and up. This is a great way to introduce dichotomous keys before using them for plant, tree, or leaf identification. It could be done the first day of class because students will be arriving with brand new school supplies. This could be a great "inquiry" activity (an activity with little or no instructions for the students that encourages them to reason things out and explore on their own) if you give students no framework, except for explaining that all questions must be answered with either a yes or no. After they create their keys, you can give them items they didn't have and ask them to place them on their keys.

Pedigree Charts

Learn how to draw a family tree.

Biology Concept: Pedigree charts

From the Junk Drawer:

☐ Whiteboard and markers (or paper and pencil)

☐ Sticky notes

☐ Poker chips (or coins)

Step 1: In a family tree, males are usually represented by squares (or rectangles), and females are represented by circles. A horizontal line represents a marriage or a union.

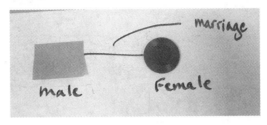

Step 2: Vertical lines represent offspring. In this example, the parents had two girls and a boy.

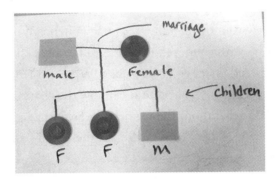

Step 3: The Roman numerals written to the side of the chart represent the generations. The parents are the first generation, and their children are the second generation.

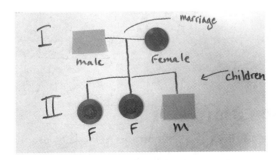

Step 4: If one of the girls had a child with a partner, the diagram would appear like this. Did they have a boy or a girl?

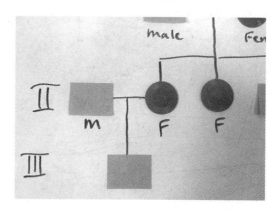

Step 5: Try to draw your own family tree on a whiteboard or large piece of paper, starting with your grandparents. You can use sticky notes to represent males and poker chips or coins to represent females. It is OK if it is not perfect; you are just trying to learn how the chart works. You will be in the third (III) generation. The framework below can give you a starting point. Add more lines for aunts, uncles, brothers, and sisters. Family trees can get large and complex.

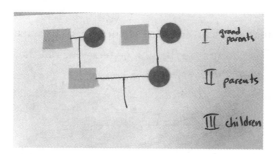

The Science Behind It

Pedigree charts are commonly called family trees. They are most commonly used with horses, show dogs, and humans. They show the relationships between grandparents, parents, and their children. They can also be used to show dominant and recessive traits (like brown eyes). Dominant traits will never skip a generation, but recessive traits can.

Science for the Ages

Family trees are fun to draw. However, they can get complicated quickly. High school students and advanced middle schoolers could add dominant and recessive traits. In that case, they would need two different colored poker chips and two different colored sticky notes.

Homemade Stethoscope

Build a stethoscope from common household items.

Biology Concepts: Stethoscope and circulatory system

Adult supervision required

From the Junk Drawer:

- ☐ Sports-drink bottle cap (or flat bottle cap and drill)
- ☐ Pliers
- ☐ Scissors
- ☐ Plastic tubing
- ☐ Electrical or clear tape
- ☐ Hot glue gun
- ☐ Balloon
- ☐ Broken pair of earbuds
- ☐ Coat hanger (optional)
- ☐ Wire cutters (optional)

You may have to get the plastic tubing from the store. You can find aquarium tubing at big-box or hardware stores. The tubing used in the pictures came from silly glasses, where a straw made it possible for someone to see the drink before tasting it.

Step 1: Take the sports-drink bottle cap and use pliers to spin the top off. This will take some effort. You could also use a flat cap, but you would need adult help to drill two holes for the tubing.

Step 2: Use the point of a pair of scissors to clean out any leftover plastic from taking the top off. Push one blade of the scissors through the opening and then spin the top while holding the scissors in place.

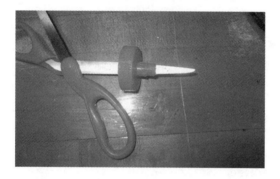

Step 3: Cut two pieces of tubing about 24 inches long. They can always be trimmed later if they're too long. Slide one end of each piece through the opening in the top of the bottle cap. The tubing needs to go through the cap but not extend beyond the bottom of the cap.

Step 4: Use tape to secure the tubing in place on the top of the bottle cap. Clear tape and electrical tape work well.

Step 5: Use hot glue to seal around the tubing in the open end of the bottle cap. Be sure that no glue gets inside the tubing.

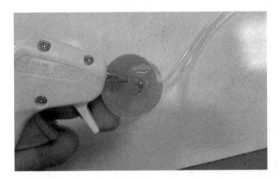

Step 6: Cut the neck off a balloon. Stretch the balloon over the open bottom of the cap. Twist the balloon tightly around the plastic tubing.

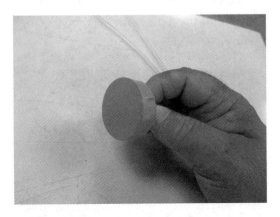

Step 7: Use more tape to secure the balloon. You want the balloon over the open end of the cap to be very tight.

Step 8: Add another piece of tape about eight inches up the tubing to hold the two pieces together. You can skip ahead to Step 13 to finish the stethoscope if you don't want to make a metal frame. It will still work without a frame, but the frame is what makes it look like a doctor's stethoscope.

Step 9 (optional): Ask an adult for help with this step. Cut the bottom of a metal coat hanger. Place your cutting tool about three fourths of an inch up the side of the hanger. For most hangers, this can be done with pliers. You can also use wire cutters, which are designed for this task. Repeat the cut on the other side of the hanger. Bend the metal piece that you have cut away from the bottom of the hanger into a V by placing the pliers in the middle of the metal piece and bending it.

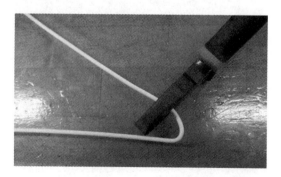

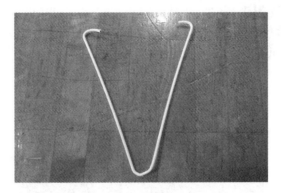

Step 10 (optional): Bend the metal piece at a right angle about three fourths of an inch from each end. Hold the V in place as you bend using the pliers. By creating these two bends in the wire, you are eliminating the possibility of the hanger going into your ear, ultimately making the device safer to use.

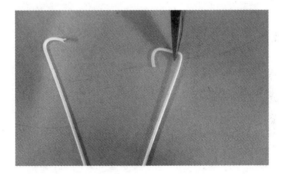

Step 11 (optional): Your finished frame should look like the picture.

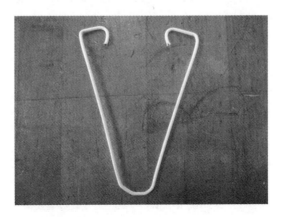

Step 12 (optional): Place the tubing along the frame and secure it with tape. The tubing needs to extend beyond the frame both on the top and the bottom of the stethoscope.

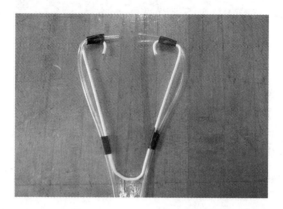

Step 13: Detach the rubber earbud sleeves from a broken pair of earbuds.

Step 14: Slide the rubber earbud sleeves over the end of the tubing. You may need to secure them with tape or hot glue, but most of them will fit snugly without reinforcement.

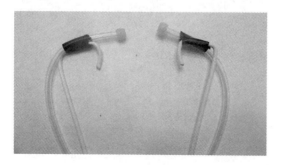

Step 15: Make your surroundings as quiet as possible by turning off all devices. Put the earbuds in your ears and place the other end on your chest. If you listen carefully, you should be able to hear your heartbeat. You may need to move the bottom end around to find the best location.

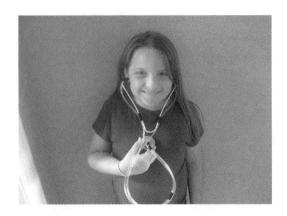

The Science Behind It

Your heart is at the center of your circulatory system. As it beats, it delivers blood loaded with oxygen and glucose to your muscles to make them work. The oxygen and glucose are used by your muscles, and the "used" blood is shuttled to the intestines to pick up more glucose and other nutrients. The blood then travels back to the heart and lungs to pick up more oxygen. This happens about once every second as you sit still. Your heart beats faster when your muscles are working harder, like when you're exercising.

The heartbeat you hear (*lubb-dupp*) is two separate sounds. The heart has four chambers, two on the input side and two on the output side. The two top chambers (one input, one output) move blood to the bottom chambers, making the *lubb* sound, the softer of the two sounds. Because it takes more effort for the larger bottom chambers to pump blood, the *dupp* sound is louder. The bottom chamber that acts as the input pushes blood to your lungs, and the bottom chamber that acts as the output pushes blood to your entire body. This happens thousands of times every day, even when you are sleeping.

Science for the Ages

Young students will need adult assistance with this activity. Upper elementary and beyond can probably build this by themselves (with help or supervision for the glue gun). In a classroom setting, you could build and use the stethoscopes. If you plan to reuse them in the future, the earbud covers should be cleaned with alcohol. What would make the most sense is to have each student bring his or her own earbuds to fit onto the already constructed stethoscopes.

Silica Gel, the Magnifier

Recycle an everyday item to make your cell phone a better magnifier

Biology Concept: Seeing small things

From the Junk Drawer:

☐ Silica gel packet
☐ Scissors
☐ Index card (or other thick paper)

☐ Pushpin
☐ Tape
☐ Cell phone with camera

Step 1: You need a silica gel pack commonly found in new shoes and new electronics. Take the scissors and snip off one corner. You want to find the largest round silica bead. If the gel pack has powdered silica in it, clean up any mess and find another packet. Most have round silica beads, but not all.

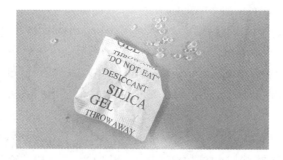

Step 2: Cut a small strip off an index card. You can actually use any thick paper, like an old birthday card or business card. Use a pushpin to create a hole in the end of the strip. Wiggle it around until it is slightly smaller than the silica bead.

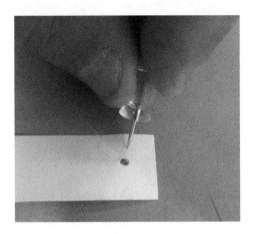

Step 3: Push the bead into the hole. This will cause the card to curve slightly in the direction you are pushing. Push the bead in until it stays in place. If it doesn't want to stay in place, poke a new hole and repeat the process.

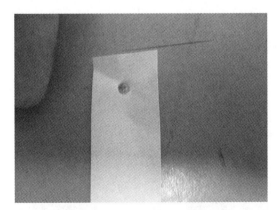

Step 4: Tape the bead directly over the camera lens on your phone. You might need to turn on the camera to determine which opening is the lens.

Step 5: Turn the phone over so you can see the display screen. The lights in the room need to be bright (or use a flashlight). Point the phone at something you want to look at. Leaves, dead bugs, and money all make interesting items to view. Once you have found something interesting, use the magnification now on the cell phone lens to make it larger. The camera will still work on your phone, so you can take a picture of it to keep. Dispose of the extra silica beads and wash your hands.

The Science Behind It

The beads are usually round, bending the light that passes through them and making a decent mini magnifying glass. When taped to a phone, they roughly double the phone's magnification; if the phone's magnification is 8×, adding the bead almost doubles that magnification to 16×. Therefore, what you see looking through it can be almost 16 times larger than the actual object.

Science for the Ages

This is safe for upper elementary age and up. One gel packet would probably suffice for the whole classroom.

Keep a close eye on younger students during this activity. The silica gel is a desiccant, meaning it will readily absorb water vapor and could cause an upset stomach or mild dehydration if swallowed. The packaging could also be a choking hazard for preschoolers.

Smartphone Microscope

Use a smartphone camera to get a glimpse at the small world around you.

Biology Concepts: Microscopes or simple magnification

From the Junk Drawer:

- ☐ Old laser pointer
- ☐ Needle-nose pliers
- ☐ Cell phone with camera
- ☐ Poster putty (or Play-Doh)
- ☐ Something to look at (dollar bill, coin, dead bug)

Step 1: You need an old laser pointer that has a lens. Some really cheap laser pointers do not have a lens, but the only way to know is to tear them apart. This activity will ruin the laser pointer, so only do it with a laser pointer that no longer works.

Use needle-nose pliers to remove the batteries, if possible. The battery compartment is usually found on the end of the pointer opposite the lens.

Step 2: Use the pliers to remove the end with the lens. Hold the pointer in one hand and the pliers in the other. Twist until it comes loose.

Step 3: If the lens doesn't fall out, carefully use the pliers to pull it out. It will be small, about two to four millimeters in diameter. You may have to bend the front end to get it out.

Step 4: Place this lens over the camera lens on a smartphone. If you are unsure where the camera is, follow these instructions. Turn on the phone's camera. Move your fingertips around until you block the camera lens. You will know when this happens because the screen will go dark. The phone shown has a light and a camera that look very similar, so check to make sure which is which.

Step 5: Secure the lens in place using poster putty. Play-Doh will also work but won't stick as long.

Step 6: You need a bright room or even a flashlight for the best results. Start with a small coin to test how well your magnifier works. Turn on the camera and place the lens directly above a coin. Slowly move the phone away from the coin until it is clear. At this distance, move the camera to see more of the coin.

Some lenses will need to be turned over to work. If the image is not any larger, go back to Step 4, turn the lens over, and try again.

The lens creates an optical zoom. Your camera also has a digital zoom. With most cameras, you can use two fingers to zoom in or out. Once you have mastered the coin, go explore leaves, bugs, and even your skin. The advantage of a camera over a traditional microscope is the ability to take pictures. You can take pictures of all of the small things around you.

The Science Behind It

The Smartphone Microscope can give you up to a 30× magnification with most lenses. It may be possible to get more or less, depending on the camera and the lens. An optical zoom is created by the lens; by adding it, you change the focusing power of the camera. The autofocus feature of the phone's camera will no longer work, however, which is why you have to move the microscope up and down to get the object into focus.

A camera has an optical zoom feature, which takes the existing picture and expands it. The picture will not be too clear when you do that. That is because the phone isn't picking up any more visual information than before. The pixels simply spread out to make the image larger. With both the optical and digital zoom, the Smartphone Microscope can give you a peek into the small world that exists around you.

Science for the Ages

This activity is perfect for all ages, though the younger ones will require adult assistance. Teachers can store the lenses in an envelope for future classes. A fun game would be to take magnified pictures of objects and have others try to guess what they are.

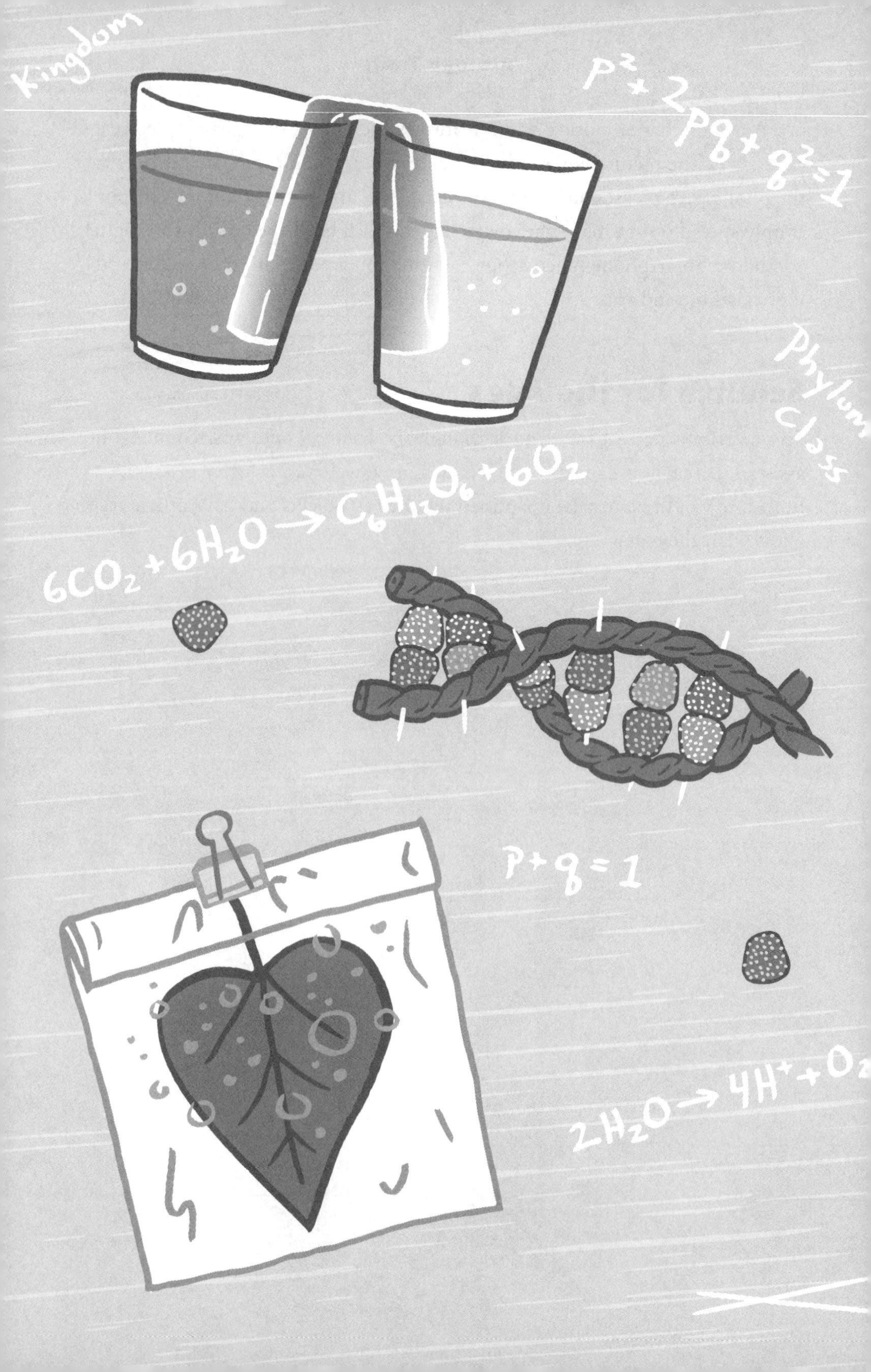

Kingdom
p²+2pq+q²=1
Phylum
Class
6CO₂+6H₂O → C₆H₁₂O₆+6O₂
p+q=1
2H₂O → 4H⁺+O₂

Glossary

Allele: A type gene that determines a genetic trait, like hair color.

Anaphase: A stage of cell division in which the chromosomes move to opposite sides of the cell to begin to make two new cells

Capillary action: The ability of water to move within a porous material

Cell: The basic unit of all living material

Cell membrane: The outer edge of a cell that protects the cell

Cell wall: The rigid barrier on the outside of a plant, fungi, or bacteria cell

Chloroplasts: Organelle inside a cell where photosynthesis takes place

Cornea: The transparent covering of the eyeball

Cytokinesis: A process that occurs at the end of cell division that creates two new daughter cells

Diffusion: A process during which substances move from a higher to lower concentration

DNA: Deoxyribonucleic acid, the hereditary material found in all living things

Dominant gene: The allele of a gene that will show if present

Gene: A unit of heredity that carries information from parent to offspring

Genetics: The branch of biology that studies genes and heredity

Interphase: The resting period between cell divisions

Meiosis: A type of cell division associated with reproduction

Metaphase: The stage of cell division where the chromosomes line up in the middle of the cell

Mitosis: A type of cell division associated with tissue growth

Neuron: A nerve cell that typically carries electrical signals to and from the brain

Nucleus: A part of the cell where most of the DNA is located

Osmosis: Process during which molecules move through a membrane

Perspiration: The process of sweating

Phenotype: The observable characteristics of a living organism

Prophase: The first stage of cell division, during which the chromosomes become visible with a microscope and the nuclear membrane dissolves

Punnett square: A square diagram that show the chances of genes being passed on to offspring

Recessive gene: An allele that might not show up as a trait if a dominant gene is present

Reflex: An action performed in response to a stimulus

Retina: The inside lining of the eye

RNA: Ribonucleic acid, it acts as a messenger carrying instruction form the DNA on how to build proteins

Semipermeable membrane: A membrane that allows material to move through it; the cell membrane is one example

Stomata: Openings in a leaf through which the leaf breathes

Sweat glands: The small tubular organisms in your body that secrete perspiration

Telophase: The final phase of cell division when new nuclei are formed

Trait: A physical characteristic that shows up in a plant or person, like brown eyes. The traits of offspring originate from genes of the parents.

Transcription: The process of copying a cell's DNA

Translation: The process of creating proteins from RNA

Transpiration: The process of water moving from roots to leaves, where it turns into water vapor

Also available from Chicago Review Press

Junk Drawer Algebra

50 Awesome Activities That Don't Cost a Thing

by Bobby Mercer

250 B/W Photos

"A book that teaches your young giftee algebra in a fun, non-stuffy way."
—*QSaltLake Magazine*

Trade Paper • 176 pages • ISBN: 978-1-64160-098-9 • $14.99 (CAN $19.99) • Ages 9 and up

Junk Drawer Geometry

50 Awesome Activities That Don't Cost a Thing

by Bobby Mercer

150 B/W Photos

"This book is full of experiments and gee-whiz coolness." —*Times Record*

Trade Paper • 192 pages • ISBN: 978-0-912777-79-5

$14.99 (CAN $19.99) • Ages 9 and up

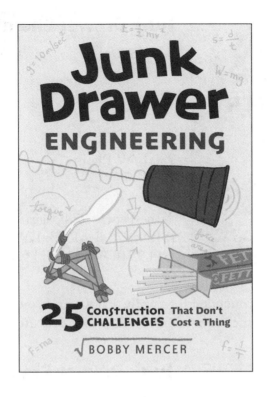

Junk Drawer Engineering

50 Construction Challenges That Don't Cost a Thing

by Bobby Mercer

420 B/W Photos

"The compilation and suggested modifications for youngsters with different backgrounds and skill sets make this particularly welcome for science teachers as well as young learners. . . . Hours of fun for STEM-inclined kids, parents, caregivers, and teachers." —*Kirkus Reviews*

Trade Paper • 224 pages • ISBN: 978-1-61373-716-3

$14.99 (CAN $19.99) • Ages 9 and up

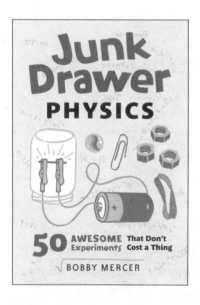